Spreading palms for Gypsies to read, beguiled rustics fail to see the plunder of their village.

Gypsies
Wanderers of the World

By Bart McDowell, *Senior Editorial Staff*
With Illustrations by Bruce Dale, *Staff Photographer*
Foreword by an English Gypsy, Clifford Lee

Prepared by the Special Publications Division, Robert L. Breeden, *Chief*
National Geographic Society, Washington, D. C.
Melvin M. Payne, *President*
Melville Bell Grosvenor, *Editor-in-Chief*
Frederick G. Vosburgh, *Editor*

GYPSIES: Wanderers of the World

By BART MCDOWELL
National Geographic Senior Editorial Staff

Photographs by BRUCE DALE
National Geographic Photographer

Published by
THE NATIONAL GEOGRAPHIC SOCIETY
MELVIN M. PAYNE, *President*
MELVILLE BELL GROSVENOR, *Editor-in-Chief*
FREDERICK G. VOSBURGH, *Editor*
GILBERT M. GROSVENOR, *Executive Editor*
  for this series
HOWARD LA FAY, *Consulting Editor*
ANGUS M. FRASER, M.A., *Consultant, Honorary*
  Assistant Editor, The Gypsy Lore Society, London
DR. JIŘÍ LÍPA, *Consultant, Czechoslovak Academy*
  of Sciences, Prague, Czechoslovakia

Prepared by
THE SPECIAL PUBLICATIONS DIVISION
ROBERT L. BREEDEN, *Editor*
DONALD J. CRUMP, *Associate Editor*
PHILIP B. SILCOTT, *Manuscript Editor*
TEE LOFTIN SNELL, *Research and Style*

Illustrations
BRYAN HODGSON, *Picture Editor*
JOSEPH A. TANEY, *Art Director*
JOSEPHINE B. BOLT, *Assistant Art Director*
URSULA PERRIN, *Design Assistant*
PAUL G. EDWARDS, JOHANNA G. FARREN,
  RONALD M. FISHER, H. ROBERT MORRISON,
  TEE LOFTIN SNELL, GERALD S. SNYDER, KYLE
  WARREN, *Picture Legends*
MARJORIE W. CLINE, JOHANNA G. FARREN,
  HELGA R. KOHL, *Picture-Legend Research*
BETTY CLONINGER, BOBBY G. CROCKETT, JOHN
  D. GARST, JR., MONICA T. WOODBRIDGE,
  Map Research and Production

Production and Printing
ROBERT W. MESSER, *Production Manager*
ANN H. CROUCH, GAIL FARMER, *Production*
  Assistants
JAMES R. WHITNEY, JOHN R. METCALFE,
  Engraving and Printing
SUZANNE J. JACOBSON, DONNA REY NAAME,
  JOAN PERRY, SANDRA A. TURNER,
  Staff Assistants
JOLENE MCCOY, VIRGINIA S. THOMPSON, *Index*

*Page 2: "Two Gypsy Children Beside a Kettle," an 1855 water-
color by Austrian artist August Pettenkofen. Page 1: Youngsters
race to catch up with a market-bound wagon at Pécs, Hungary. These Lovári Gypsies wished the author and his party
"Bahtalo drom! Lucky road!" Bookbinding: Detail by Bobby
G. Crockett after decorated Gypsy caravan shown on page 34.*

PAGE 2: GRAPHISCHEN SAMMLUNG "ALBERTINA," VIENNA

*A*ll outdoors her playground,
a Gypsy girl nibbles a blade of grass
near her family's camp on the
Neckar River in southern Germany.

Foreword

I AM A GYPSY, born in a caravan. This book tells much about me and my people and about a long journey I made to India, that fabulous land where my forebears originated.

I had always known that someday I would make this trip. We call it *dukkeripen*—saying the future. But I confess I did not recognize that future one summer day when a tall American stranger came to my home. He introduced himself as Bart McDowell, and in this book he reports what happened.

That meeting was the start of a fantastic magic-carpet journey which took us through Western and Eastern Europe and on through the Near East to the Indus watershed. Along the way I met my people, the Gypsies, met them in poverty and in prosperity, and found what I'd long suspected: that the world over, we are fundamentally the same. Wherever we met, we had in common our Romany—our ancient language. Sometimes it would be only an odd word, sometimes many words. But to me the most important discovery was the affinity I felt with the other *Rom*. I was often surprised to see Gypsies who looked amazingly like relatives and friends of mine back home in England. Sometimes a gesture caught my eyes; sometimes it was a physical resemblance, the angle of a jaw line, a face thrown into relief beside a lonely campfire. But most of all, it was the black Gypsy eyes that reminded me of so many Gypsy people I know.

All of us, I found, had much the same problem with those *gorgios*—non-Gypsies—who want to force their ways upon us without realizing that we want no such thing, and with self-styled "experts" who so often portray us either as happy children of nature living on hedgehogs roasted in clay, or as thieves menacing society. I think my friend Bart McDowell has used the best technique: He has let us speak for ourselves. In this book Bart and photographer Bruce Dale, the ubiquitous Bruce, show us as we are. Their record presents Gypsy life in change: Here a motorcar replaces a horse, there a government bans the roving life.

I felt the tug of change myself during our journey, so that today, along with my craft of knife-grinding, I take paying guests on camping trips. We are a resourceful and resilient people who have adapted to other changes in the past thousand years. We ourselves never change. It is hard to alter a people who are content with their lot, and wish only to be what they are and always have been—Gypsies. As Englishman George Borrow, who wrote romantically of us, said, "There's night and day ... sun, moon, and stars ... wind on the heath. Life is very sweet...."

CLIFFORD LEE

Contents

Tattered canvas covers the caravan of a wandering Gypsy stopped by the side of the road near the village of Caiuti, Rumania.

Gypsy fortune-teller: symbol of her mysterious folk.

The 'Outlandysshe People'

S HE TOLD FORTUNES, this English Gypsy called Madam Thorney, and she held my right hand tight. I expected her to study my open palm; instead, she searched my face.

"You are writing something," Madam Thorney said at once. "A book, perhaps. And you are planning a journey."

I studied this fortune-teller with puzzled respect: her arresting, heavy-lidded eyes and her strong, gentle features — a face suggesting nose-jewels and saris. I had never before laid eyes on Madam Thorney, nor she on me. Here I sat in her trailer, or caravan, one of hundreds of Americans at Epsom Downs for Derby Day. Yet unlike so many others, I had not come for the horses but to see Gypsies like Madam Thorney herself.

"Yes, a very long journey," she said. "Where *are* you going?"

I hedged. How could I tell her all my plan? I would soon be crossing the English Channel and driving overland to India, and with me would travel a British Gypsy couple whom Madam Thorney herself might know. We had elaborate plans. We would camp out when necessary. And we would visit other Gypsies along the way — settled ones, nomadic ones, flamenco dancers, fortune-tellers, violinists, coppersmiths. That very day in London I had packed away a money belt, for I also expected to meet some Gypsy thieves.

"I could tell you more with the five-pound reading. You have a question?" she asked. I had absolutely no questions worth five pounds sterling. "What *could* you give?" she asked. "It must be given with goodwill, you know, or the money will do me no good." My goodwill just stretched to a one-pound note, so Madam Thorney took a crystal ball out of her apron pocket — a small one, barely larger than a walnut. She fondled it, then quite ignored it, keeping her splendid dark eyes right on me.

"Now your work," she began. "Be careful. Beware of things others may write down or tell you. Write only what you find for yourself."

With that advice, Madam Thorney easily earned her pound. And I commend her crystalline counsel to anyone who tries to study Gypsies. For centuries these curious people have confounded philologists, anthropologists, ethnologists, sociologists, musicologists, historians. Gypsies resist formal study; ask them questions and you often get answers fanciful or false — or no answer at all. Evasion is their tactic of survival. Just as coloring protects game, so an air of romantic mystery has camouflaged these least domesticated of civilized peoples. We can only pity a scholar whom Gypsies have deliberately fooled. Some of the most beautifully documented research often contains footnoted nonsense. Madam Thorney, consciously or not, had ably served the cause of truth. She was wise. Perhaps, I conceded, she was more than wise. For I could not explain her amazing insight into my work and travel plans. Not then. Later, when we reached the camel routes of old Persia, I would gain some insights of my own into Madam Thorney's crystal ball. But that is ahead of the story.

We should start long ago, when as a boy I first read the book *Raggle Taggle.* In it Irish author and educator Walter Starkie told how he took his facile fiddle and went vagabonding among the Gypsies of Hungary and Rumania. I was hooked.

The glamor flamed higher when I saw and heard my first *Carmen.* And who could resist Victor Hugo's dancing Esmeralda in *The Hunchback of Notre Dame* — "her round and graceful arms held high above her head, slender, quick and active as any wasp."

Through the years I met other sorts of Gypsies: a leather craftsman in California, a mender of driveways in Virginia, horse traders in Spain, dancing-bear leaders in Turkey, kettle menders wandering the Peruvian Andes. Once, in the paneled propriety of San Francisco's Bohemian Club, I met one of America's leading cardiologists, Dr. Louis Krasno, whose father and grandfather played violin in a famous Rumanian Gypsy ensemble, and served in turn as its *primás,* or leader. "Make Gypsies settle down?" remarked the versatile Dr. Krasno, who is himself a violinist. "Well, it's being done, but it's a bit like harnessing a lion to a plow."

His fellow Gypsies in the United States would concur, especially those among the 50,000 to 100,000 who flow like ocean currents throughout the land. Though some deported European Gypsies began roaming the Americas in the 17th century, most immigrated late in the 19th century

"You are writing something...and you are planning a journey," Madam Thorney (left) told author Bart McDowell at England's Epsom Downs. A younger fortune-teller, Emily, peers into the future for photographer Bruce Dale. She predicted the outcome of the Derby, but her choice—Approval—finished seventh.

from Russia and Serbia, and from the same Hungarian-Rumanian areas that the Krasnos once called home.

Until the 1930's most of them wandered, trading horses, mending pots and pans, telling fortunes. The depression and the automobile pushed them into the cities. Now they do odd jobs—with an occasional touch of swindle, some police say—tell fortunes, or draw welfare checks, concentrating in such cities as Los Angeles, Chicago, Toledo, Boston, New York, and Portland, Oregon.

Those who travel swoop as mood suggests from Canada to Mexico. Their names vary enormously, reflecting family origins throughout Europe—or their own inventive preferences.

Different as each Gypsy may be, all have something spontaneous in common. Despite restrictions, the Gypsy has defeated the humdrum life. He seems the last happy grasshopper in a world of ants. We have to envy this Huckleberry Finn who often skips school and who doesn't have to wash or follow any prim rules of piety or punctuality.

So I continued to read, and I began a correspondence with the amazing Dr. Dora E. Yates, Honorary Secretary of the Gypsy Lore Society in Liverpool and editor of its journal.

As fate would have it, work took me to the port of Liverpool, and I made a special point of visiting Dr. Yates at the university there. Dr. Yates—called the *Rawnie,* or "Great Lady," by British Gypsies—was nearly 90, the last surviving link with the 19th-century philologists who first studied British Gypsies. I frankly expected to meet a feeble relic. Instead, I found a brisk, firm-stepping lady with a spirit to match her lively subject.

We talked at length about Romany—the language of the Gypsies—and of its Sanskrit roots and of a word it has given the English language, "pal," which I think reflects the Gypsies' own companionable warmth.

Dr. Yates's dark eyes sparkle when she talks about her early Gypsy adventures among the Boswells, Locks, Woods, Lees, and all the other English Gypsy families. In the early years of the 20th century she helped the great Gypsiologist and linguist John Sampson compile his grammar and dictionary of the Welsh Gypsy dialect. "Of course, I could only help after my work in the university library was complete at five each afternoon," Dr. Yates recalled. "And not until I had mastered both English and foreign Romany did Dr. Sampson introduce me to his Gypsy friends."

Gypsies took the pretty brunette Rawnie into the confidence of their tents and horse-drawn caravans, told her their folktales, sang her their songs, and even taught her how to tell fortunes. Once, when some of her Gypsy friends in Liverpool were ill and could not work, Dora Yates borrowed a gaudy shawl, a begging apron enriched with pockets, and a basket of clothespins for hawking. Then off she went to fashionable Victoria Park, knocking on doors to *dukker* — or tell fortunes.

"I easily disguised my voice," she said, "and adopted the solemn, mysterious tones of these fortune-tellers."

She knew all the convincing catchwords: "You've got no common hand, girl....There's luck in your lovely face, lady....You'll call to rememberment all your long life what the poor Gypsy girl tells you this day."

So Dora Yates, folklorist and philologist, dukkered "both mistress and maid, and foretold for each of them a fortune which made their eyes goggle with delighted surprise, and must have given them happy dreams that night." She also sold her basket of clothespins — and grossed a quick 27 shillings for her Gypsy friends. "I thought to myself," said Dora Yates, "that never in my life before had I earned money so easily or given so much pleasure."

Years later, Dr. Yates even bought a horse and a barrel-topped caravan for summertime camping with Romanies. The horse she eventually sold at a £4 profit. "So," she says, "I pride myself on being a good *graiengeri* — horse trader."

"Before I leave," I asked at last, "do you know any interesting Liverpool Gypsies I might visit?"

"Yes," said Dr. Yates without a pause. "A knife grinder named Clifford Lee. An unusual man. Entirely self-educated."

The Rawnie had known four generations of Lees, beginning with Clifford's grandfather Ithal in 1908. She still recalled the "lighthearted gaiety and profound wisdom" of Ithal Lee.

"And Clifford Lee comes from the same stock," she added. "He wanted his son Kenneth to attend school

Journey to the Gypsy homeland begins in Liverpool with a visit to a scholar known to Gypsies as the "Great Lady," and a debate in the House of Lords at London.

regularly, so he bought a house and moved into it. While Kenneth went to school, Clifford borrowed books from the local library to teach himself. The first time I met him, he actually spoke Latin. He especially likes the Greek philosophers. I think his son's success inspired Clifford with his own reading. Young Kenneth became the first Gypsy to graduate from any British university."

Dora Yates was particularly pleased with Kenneth because he was her protégé at the University of Liverpool. "He now teaches geography in an Australian college," she said proudly.

*M*odern-day Carmen dances in her
family's cafe, built inside a cave on Sacro
Monte in Granada. Above, the
raven-haired Andalusian sips a glass of wine.
Gypsies and Spanish workers once occupied
about 1,200 such caves, but flooding
in 1963 ruined all except a dozen or so.

PENSIVE MATRON IN CZECHOSLOVAKIA RUMANIAN VILLAGERS ENGLISH YOUTH AT THE APPLEBY FAIR

In the world of Gypsies, a world of difference: An exuberant Rumanian salutes visitors at her village; an Indian woman peeks shyly at the photographer.

In her firm hand Dr. Yates wrote down Clifford Lee's address for me. I found the place, a neat corner row house in the Liverpool suburb of Maghull, just as a panel van turned into the drive. Thus I met Clifford and Sheila Lee at almost the same time.

"From Dr. Yates? The Rawnie?" Clifford Lee asked. "Well, you must come in. No, my hand is dirty from grinding knives. We can shake hands soon as I have me a wash. Sorry, but when my hands are clean, I'm not making money."

"Could I get you a cup of tea?" asked Sheila Lee. We got acquainted over some fancy red-and-gold-trimmed cups. ("Gypsies never use white china. It's bad luck. White is for mourning," Cliff explained.) The house, though small, was attractively furnished, busy with bright designs, books, china, lace doilies. Everything sparkled in pillow-plumping order—all except some catalogues Cliff Lee had strewn across a sofa.

"Ignore my disorder," he said. "I'm reading about Land-Rovers. I'd like to sell our house and go back on the road. My son lives in Australia now, and my two daughters are grown young women. We no longer need a house...." Cliff Lee got a faraway look. "We could get one of these caravan-campers and drive most of the way to Australia."

"How would you pay for the trip?" I asked.

He laughed. "Gypsies can always manage. I'd grind knives." I had a sudden thought about knife grinders I'd seen in the Near East, people earning barely enough to fill their own bellies, let alone gasoline tanks.

AS I THINK BACK NOW, it seems strange that I asked Cliff about his personal finances so soon after meeting him. But there was something in his manner that made him instantly an old friend. We talked away the afternoon and a large part of the evening while Sheila brought us food. Cliff told of his childhood and how his mother taught him to beg. "We'd be in a crowd, and my mother would say, 'Come away from the nice lady. Don't bother the dear lady. *Mong, chavo, mong!*' That was Romany, and it meant 'Beg, boy, beg!'

MOTHER AND CHILD IN HUNGARY   VEILED INDIAN WOMAN   HUNGARIAN BOY AND PET

*"Different as each . . . may be, all have something spontaneous in common," says
the author, who calls the Gypsy "the last happy grasshopper in a world of ants."*

"I still beg," said Cliff. "Oh, not from friends, don't worry. But see this
suit of clothes." He took one from the closet to show its Savile Row label.
"I begged it off a man when I sharpened his lawn mower."

We talked about Cliff's Gypsy kinfolk and their wonderful names:
Cinderella, Reservoira, 'Nation (short for Carnation), "Old Jumpy" (a
man named Jump-the-Brook), Wisdom Smith ("the only Gypsy gold
dealer in Britain"), Cliff's Uncle Bias, and Old Bohemius: "I shouldn't
mention *his* name," said Cliff. "It's bad luck to speak the name of someone dead."

I tried to get Cliff Lee's reaction to all the cliché questions people ask:
Is there a King of the Gypsies? What's the Gypsy religion like? Do they
steal children?

"As you know, there isn't any king," said Cliff. "Oh, one man claimed to
be, a few years back." Cliff's brow creased and his deep voice grated:
"The world's biggest unhung charlatan. Now, mind you, if an old Gypsy
man dies somewhere and his family wants a nice burial, they may tell the
gorgios, non-Gypsies, he was a king—like a chief, you know.

"That religion question—I was baptized a Roman Catholic in Ireland,
and as a boy I went to church often, but only to other baptisms. The
priests used to give a baptized child a bit of money. I recall once when I
was a boy we went to eight churches one Sunday and got the same infant
baptized each time. Different names in every church. A borrowed baby.

"But here in England most Gypsies are Church of England. In Scotland,
Presbyterian. And in Turkey, Moslems. We're what the country is.

"Now that story about stealing children. I keep hearing it, of course.
But Gypsies have no shortage of their own. We're a fertile people."

We drank gallons of tea. ("I'm a virtual tea-totaler," said Cliff Lee,
whose only serious vice is punning.) Over the cups our talk ranged the
world. Cliff recalled horses his father had bought and sold, and Gypsy
friends who had broken wild colts (". . . he was riding that two-year-old
bareback and the froth was bubbling up around his knees . . ."). He described light-footed dancers (". . . oh, he could dance on eggs, that boy;

Emerging from northwest India about a thousand years ago, Gypsies traced a path of legend and romance across Asia and Europe. (Heavier lines show major routes.) Words the migrants borrowed in their wanderings give evidence that they stopped in northern Persia and among Armenian and Greek-speaking people of Byzantium. Europe's earliest record describing people who sound like Gypsies appears in writings of a monk at Mount Athos, Greece, in 1100. Archives and travelers' accounts show them in Crete, Corfu, and the Balkans before 1350. In 1417 a band of the dark-skinned, ragged vagrants, led by a fancily dressed "Duke" and a "Count," arrived near Hamburg, Germany. Within a century, most Europeans knew them as vagabond fortune-tellers, singers, dancers, beggars, and cunning tricksters.

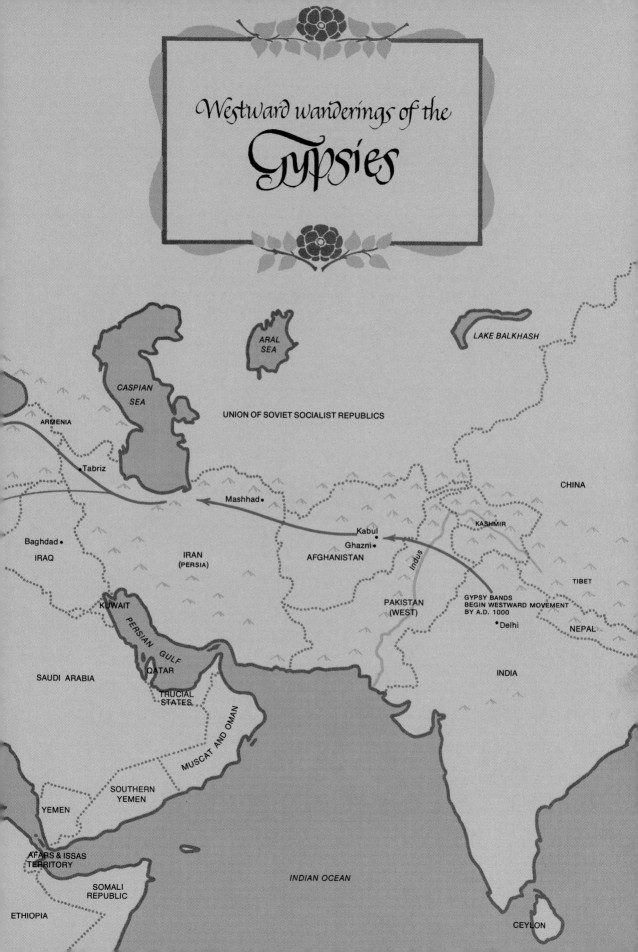

Westward wanderings of the Gypsies

LAKE BALKHASH

ARAL
SEA

CASPIAN
SEA

UNION OF SOVIET SOCIALIST REPUBLICS

ARMENIA

Tabriz

CHINA

Mashhad

KASHMIR

Kabul

Ghazni

AFGHANISTAN

Indus

Baghdad

IRAQ

IRAN
(PERSIA)

TIBET

KUWAIT

PERSIAN GULF

QATAR

SAUDI ARABIA

TRUCIAL
STATES

PAKISTAN
(WEST)

GYPSY BANDS
BEGIN WESTWARD MOVEMENT
BY A.D. 1000

Delhi

NEPAL

INDIA

MUSCAT AND OMAN

SOUTHERN
YEMEN

YEMEN

AFARS & ISSAS
TERRITORY

SOMALI
REPUBLIC

ETHIOPIA

INDIAN OCEAN

CEYLON

thin as a whiplash, he was . . ."). And he talked about the way people in Liverpool reacted to his own brunet, lean-faced, foreign appearance. "Other Gypsies know me for a Gypsy, of course," said Cliff. "But gorgios seem uncertain. 'Are you Spanish?' they ask. Or, 'Are you Jewish or Italian?' I always just say yes, whatever they ask. But Gypsies can usually tell the *tacho rat,* or true blood." His credentials were perfect: "Born in a caravan, I was, and my father before me born in a tent. Used a horse collar for a crib. And as a *tikno* — a small boy — I was suckled by a mare. Literally, suckled: the foal on one side and me on the other."

Life in a house now seemed drab, Cliff admitted, but each summer he returned to the free life of his youth, taking his family to camp in New Forest, near Southampton. "The world throbs with life," said Cliff. "But it takes me ten days in the caravan to begin feeling its rhythm again. In a house you sleep all night without knowing what the weather is like until you open the blinds next morning. But in a caravan you hear the rain on a canvas roof. You know when the birds wake up. Living in a house, away from the sun, I've grown all fish-belly white."

He told how Gypsy families bought a new *vardo,* or caravan, in the old days: "You know, the kind built of penny-farthing boards: boards the *width* of a penny and a farthing. Some of those vardos were elaborate — wood carving, gold leaf, everything. Well, the Gypsies would go to the dealer in the dark of night, and one man would go inside the vardo with a lighted candle. If anyone outside could see even the smallest chink of light, the sale was off. A vardo had to be completely tight."

FROM OLD-FASHIONED CARAVANS we returned to Cliff's catalogues. On his proposed trip to Australia he would go through India. "Do you agree that India is the Gypsy homeland?" I asked. Cliff nodded. "Many scholars have told us so. And I wager they're right. The Gypsies themselves, as you know, had no knowledge of their true origins. When I was working as a ratcatcher here at the port, I used to board ships from every country. Well, one day I listened to some coolies from India. They were speaking Hindi and I could actually understand some of their words — the same as my own Romany. Words like *pani* for 'water' and *bal* for 'hair.' Yes, I've always wanted to visit India. I guess it's my spiritual home."

An idea began to take shape in my mind — an idea as wild as the old Gypsy life. "On this trip you want to make to Australia," I said, "if you could drive overland to India, you'd be tracing back the old migratory routes of the first Gypsies." Cliff nodded. "Well, if you could find someone to buy your gasoline, could you stand to have some company?" Cliff's eyes widened. (At least the right one did; Cliff Lee is blind in his left eye.) "You wouldn't have to grind knives to make money, so you could make the trip faster," I said.

"And we could visit Gypsies along the way," Cliff put in. "Mind you, my Romany follows the rules of English grammar — but we can still understand a lot of words used by Gypsies on the Continent, even though they follow other language forms."

"We would need pictures, so we'd have to take along a truly sensitive photographer," I said.

"How long would the trip take?" Cliff asked. I had no idea. Where were the main migration routes? Did passable roads follow the same patterns today? What seasons were best for crossing the mountains and deserts?

The whole heady notion seemed impossibly big, yet intriguing: a trip that would take an authentic Gypsy back to his ancestral source. We might even help solve some of the mysteries and settle some of the arguments that surround Gypsies all over the world.

Sheila Lee had little to say during that first visit. She smiled, served us food, and did the dishes with some help from her daughters Greta and Angela. Like a good Gypsy wife, Sheila deferred completely to her husband; she even stirred his tea for him. Yet she was not a Gypsy by blood, Cliff told me, but the pretty blue-eyed daughter of an Irish butcher whom Cliff had met while traveling in Ireland in the 1940's. With Gypsy ardor he had wooed and wed her against the noisy protests of both their families. Thereafter Sheila had learned Gypsy ways and words, so that every person in the British Isles who claims Romany blood—perhaps 10,000 souls, including all the Lees—accepted her as a proper Gypsy wife and mother. And now from her Irish eyes and Celtic blush I saw that she liked our wild idea.

A good thing she did. On our journey to India, Sheila sewed buttons on our clothes and fattened us with her campfire cooking—but she also did far more. Gypsies are a wary and secretive lot, especially when approached by male strangers. Sheila's presence vouched for our honorable intentions.

It took almost a year for our reverie to turn into concrete plans. We consulted history books and highway maps, and found the idea physically possible.

"A trip like that has never been done before," said Angus M. Fraser, Honorary Assistant Editor of the Gypsy Lore Society. "Walter Starkie has covered most of the terrain, but not on one trip. And there have been others who followed the Gypsy trail a long way, but not right back to its source." Mr. Fraser encouraged us with good advice.

Professor Starkie himself, now President of the Gypsy Lore Society, was jubilant. "I'm so pleased you're doing something with Clifford Lee. He seems the perfect modern Gypsy. Such a wonderful family."

Eden River in northwest England murmurs past Gypsy Clifford Lee, his wife Sheila, and daughters Greta and Angela. Cliff, a knife grinder, and Sheila accompanied author McDowell and photographer Dale to India on their Gypsy hunt.

Works of scholars in a dozen countries made up our reading lists. Thus we pursued an academic detective story of the 18th century, when Europeans stumbled upon their first clues to Gypsy origins. The sages learned, in fact, much the way Cliff Lee did when he overheard coolies speaking Hindi.

A Vienna newspaper, for example, published a garbled item in the 1760's about a preacher named Stephen Vali, who, as a student at the University of Leiden, "was intimately acquainted with some young Malabars [and] observed, that their native language bore a great affinity to that spoken by the Gipsies. . . ."

ℒengthening shadows precede a British Gypsy and his caravan on the road to Appleby. Each June thousands of Gypsies and hundreds of farmers gather in the Eden Valley town for the New Fair, largely to buy, sell, and trade horses.

This story came into the hands of a German scholar, Heinrich M. G. Grellmann, who wrote in 1783, "The origin of the Gipsies has remained a perfect philosopher's stone till now." He then speculated that Vali's young "Malabars" might be "Bramins sons, whose language was ... Shanscritt.... The difficulty will subside ... when I come to examine ... the Gipsey and Hindostan languages." Grellmann did so and concluded that the Gypsy homeland was "no other than Hindostan" — India.

Other scholars made the same discovery. Nineteenth-century philologists like August F. Pott and Franz Xavier von Miklosich began speculating on Gypsy migrations. About A.D. 1000, they noted, the Aryan dialects of India were changing into the forms heard today in the subcontinent. The Romany tongue in Europe included some, but not all, of those changes. Gypsies therefore must have left the lands of the Indus River watershed about a thousand years ago, they reasoned.

OTHER QUESTIONS remained open. Why did the first Gypsies leave India? Men could only guess. Perhaps they were carried away by invaders, or left because of famines, social discontent, maybe even religious vows — no proof survived. But linguists, turned detectives, could trace the Gypsy itinerary by the words the wanderers picked up along the way and added to their own language.

Romany, as Dr. Sampson said, comes "... scented with an aroma from the East. Thus, in the Gypsies' speech heard here in England, their *rashai,* or parson, descends from *rishi,* the venerable tonsured anchorite of Sanskrit literature, the *Rai* and the *Rawnie* [meaning "gentleman" and "lady"] claim kinship with the Rajah and Ranee of India.... Persia gave our Gypsies their words for silk and wool and wax, and in Iranian lands they first heard *dâriav* for 'sea' and 'ocean.' In Byzantine Greece they found their *drom,* or road, and their *foros,* or market, and learned their words for heaven and time, for lead and copper, horseshoe and kettle, for table and chair, hat and shoes, goose, dove, and peacock.... Thus ... you will find in the language of the Gypsies the true history of this people and of their wanderings."

From the Indian subcontinent the Gypsies moved first into Persian-speaking regions — Afghanistan and Iran. Then, Sampson believed, the trail forked. One group headed south and west toward Syria and North Africa, picking up Arabic words. Others turned north and then west, borrowing Armenian and Byzantine Greek words as they went. By the 14th century, linguistic guesswork about their route gives way to eye-witness documents stored in castles and churches of the Balkan peninsula.

After a quiet period along the Danube — many Gypsies were slaves in Rumania, for example — bands of the wanderers flamboyantly invaded the rest of Europe. Records show them near Hamburg in 1417, at Augsburg in southern Germany in 1418, Rome in 1422, Paris in 1427, and in Scotland in 1505. Everywhere, they made a living and a reputation telling fortunes, begging, and stealing.

Each country gave them a distinctive name. They were called *Athíngani* in Greece, Heathens in the Netherlands, Bohemians in France, and Tartars in Germany. The Moors of North Africa called them *Charami,* or robbers. Hungarians sometimes referred to them as "Pharaoh's people" — much as the English knew them as Egyptians. Gradually, though, the

English nicked the name to Gypsy, and in the Balkans and western Europe the names stabilized into words of a ring similar to that of Athíngani: *Atzigan, Cigani, Zingani, Tsygany, Zigeuner, Zingari, Zincali.* Yet the Gypsies of Europe have a single word for themselves—*Rom.* In their tongue it meant originally "a man of our own race." From it comes the word *Romani,* Anglicized to Romany.

No one today knows how many of this ethnic group survive across the world. Census takers confuse them with other sorts of wanderers and migrant workers, and Gypsies themselves mistrust any official with a clipboard. Other demographers classify Gypsies as Romanies only when they retain their old language, and, increasingly, the young are forgetting the Romany tongue. Finally come the policies of various governments. The largest Gypsy populations live in Communist countries, where officials sometimes claim to have solved their "Gypsy problem" through assimilation programs. In any case, the expert estimates range wide: Romanies may number anywhere from one million to ten million worldwide.

In each country along our route we planned to sample the history as well as the present-day customs of the Gypsies. In Britain we began the story with April 22, 1505, when the accounts of the Lord High Treasurer of Scotland record a payment of £7 "to the Egyptianis [by] the Kingis command...." They indeed claimed "Little Egypt" as their home, just as they had on the Continent; and their "Lord," Anthony Gagino, even convinced Scottish King James IV that his band was making a pilgrimage through all Christendom under a special Papal command.

Soon old ledgers showed payments of coin to "Egypcion" and "Gipcy" dancers and jugglers. But by the time of Henry VIII, Gypsy behavior had become intolerable. A royal act banned any further immigration of the "outlandysshe People callynge themselfes Egyptians" and ordered those already in the country to leave since they "had comytted many and haynous Felonyes...."

A few years later, in *The Fyrst Boke of the Introduction of Knowledge* by Andrew Borde, Gypsies appeared as "swarte and ... [disguised] in theyr apparel, contrary to other nacions, they be lyght fingerd and ... have litle maner ... yet they be pleasant daunsers.... Yf there be any man [that] wyl learne parte of theyr speche, Englyshe and Egipt speche foloweth." Dr. Borde's list of Gypsy sentences was the first record in English of the Romany language.

Appleby campers invade prohibited grounds after overflowing areas authorized for their use. Scare signs in pastures nearby discourage trespassing.

In 1554 Henry's daughter Queen Mary—"Bloody Mary"—outlawed "certain Persons calling themselves Egyptians" because of "their old accustomed devilish and naughty Practices." Gypsies were required to leave England within 40 days. The penalty for staying was death, though children under 13 and any who would take up good behavior and "lawful Work" were excepted. The law was never rigidly enforced; some courts dodged it and its grisly gallows by chartering boats to deport Gypsies.

In the time of Mary's half sister Elizabeth, the realm could count as many Gypsies as Britain claims today. Royal patience ceased. By an act of 1562 the Gypsy way of life once again became a criminal offense. I showed the old law's provisions to Clifford Lee. He laughed, a bit feloniously I thought, and said darkly that I was about to run some risk myself: Any persons who for one month "at once or at several times" stayed in the company of Gypsies and imitated "their Apparel, Speech, or other Behaviour, shall...be deemed...Felons; and shall therefore suffer Pains of Death...."

Next time I saw him, Cliff said, "Now about imitating our apparel...." and presented me with a proper Gypsy *diklo,* or scarf. "You tie it around your neck this way," he said. "First over, then under. Not at all like a noose, you see."

Cliff's gallows humor notwithstanding, a number of 16th-century travelers were hanged for keeping company with Gypsies. Others were hanged for different reasons. "An ancestor of mine," said Cliff, "the earliest one Dr. Yates could find, was Abraham Wood. He and his half brother were hanged in 1737 at Gloucester for highway robbery."

CLIFF at last assured me I had nothing to fear. "Our old Gypsy Acts were repealed in 1783 by your friend King George III," he said with a poker face. "That's not to say life grew easy. Take my own grandfather. He was once coming back from a horse fair in Cheshire, and he pulled a turnip out of a farmer's field to eat it. For that crime he was arrested and sent away for a calendar month. Mind you, the British are a fair people and would have done the same to anyone. Though perhaps they were a bit more strict with Gypsies."

I had seen British fairness in action one afternoon in 1968 during a visit to the House of Lords. Grattan Puxon, the articulate young secretary of Britain's Gypsy Council, had suggested that I take note of their Lordships' business: the third and final reading of the Caravan Sites Bill, legislation to encourage the building of trailer parks "for the use of gipsies and other persons of nomadic habit."

I looked about the august neo-Gothic chamber and recognized no Gypsies among the visitors. Yet, I think the Lords of Little Egypt would have felt quite splendidly at home with the dark paneling, stained glass, escutcheons, brasswork, woolsack, wigs, and leather benches.

Debate at this stage of the bill was brief. The government's spokesman, Lord Kennet, rose to commend Lord Wade, the bill's sponsor in the House of Lords, for his work in piloting through a measure designed to achieve a "reconciliation between Gypsies and the larger number of the population." After a few more formalities the bill would become the law, "enacted by the Queen's most Excellent Majesty."

Author of the new law was Eric Lubbock, an energetic young member of the House of Commons from Orpington in Kent. "We must not overstate the results," said Mr. Lubbock when I congratulated him that day. "We still need funds to help the local governments provide sites. But at least the Government is now committed to do more."

Our conversation turned to the Gypsy problem in Mr. Lubbock's own Kent constituency. "Kent, you may know, has Britain's greatest concentration of Gypsies," he said. "More than 300 families, according to our 1965 survey."

That year the Ministry of Housing and Local Government judged the total population of British "travelers" to be 15,000—but here they included other folk known as tinkers and mumpers—all manner of non-Gypsy migrant families who spend their lives in tents and trailers.

"Kent is an important agricultural area," Mr. Lubbock continued. "And Gypsies provide seasonal labor." He ticked off the seasons: In spring and early summer Gypsies tie young hop plants to poles; later, they gather cherries; in autumn they harvest the hops. Through the winter, when no field work is available, they resort to "car-breaking" — not car thefts, as I first assumed, but the breaking up of cars for scrap.

"An untidy business," Mr. Lubbock noted, "that most of their neighbors resent. So people often try to keep the Gypsies moving."

Thus, "the Gypsy problem" concerns a family's place to camp. People always on the move cannot send youngsters to school or free themselves from a marginal existence.

At Mr. Lubbock's suggestion I traveled out to the London Borough of Bromley, a suburban area carved out of Kent in 1965. Bromley has provided a permanent £16,000-site for 12 caravans, with stores, washrooms, hot water, and electricity. Each family pays £2 ($4.80) a week in rent, and the children go to school.

"You should have seen the Gypsy camp here at Corke's Meadow a few years ago," said Mr. F. S. Houldsworth, Borough Housing Manager. "A hundred families in huts and vans, and scrap lying around everywhere." Today the spot has a view of hills and trees. "And it adjoins the tip. Gypsies often tot the tip." A tip is a dump; totting it means combing it for salvage.

"Were the caravans *really* clean?" asked Cliff next time I saw him. I assured him they were, that the roofs sprouted TV antennas and the windowsills glinted with fancy bone china. "Ah," said Cliff, "then *our* people are using the site! Mind you, I have nothing against tinkers and mumpers, but they're just not my people."

I had seen a colony of Irish tinkers the same day only about two miles away, a tousled, noisy band — long on litter and short on soap — parked smack on the highway right-of-way.

"They have their own argot," Cliff continued. "Ancient Celtic it is, with a few Romany words picked up over the centuries, quite a different language from ours. They've been living on the roads of Britain longer than we have. But please," Cliff added, trying hard not to be snobbish, "don't call them 'Gypsies.'" I promised. And so I use the word "Gypsy" to mean a person of Romany origin — Cliff Lee and all his kind — whether he lives on the move or settled in a house, whether he still speaks Romany or remembers only a few words. "Gorgio" means everyone else.

"September Morn" in June on the Eden River: A Gypsy girl steps demurely into her bath.

The inclusion of non-Romany travelers, I suspect, has caused Clifford Lee to steer clear of membership in the Gypsy Council, Mr. Puxon's activist group.

Mr. Puxon, a highly effective humanitarian ("though a gorgio," Cliff observes), has organized more than a dozen Gypsy schools and a spate of lively protests against oppressive and archaic laws. At the Epsom racetrack in 1969, when local authorities threatened to ban Gypsy campers on Derby Day, Mr. Puxon brought dozens of caravans across police lines. "Gypsies have camped here in 'The Dip' for two centuries," he said. The authorities nimbly retreated, and the Gypsies remained.

But anyone who wants to organize Gypsies must contest romantic notions long held by English-speaking people. As early as the 17th century, playwrights were inventing Gypsy roles for the stage. Shakespeare put them into metered verse; Ben Jonson published his *Masque of the Metamorphosd Gypsies;* and Samuel Pepys recorded in his diary a Gypsy fortune-teller ("She got ninepence of me") whose prophecy that he would be asked for a loan proved, 12 days later, "to be so true." William Wordsworth deplored them as "wild outcasts of society." But in the 19th century that very wild-game quality became an attraction in the books of big George Borrow, the "bourgeois Byron" in the apt phrase of one scholar. As "Romany Rye" ("Gypsy Gentleman"), Borrow fumigated the Gypsy reputation so that the most Victorian person—young Queen Victoria herself—wrote of meeting "such a nice set of Gipsies" camped beside a road near her home, "so quiet, so affectionate to one another, so discreet, not at all forward or importunate . . . so unlike the gossiping fortune-telling race-gipsies. . . ."

"This romantic public attitude has done the Gypsy little good," says Grattan Puxon.

Perhaps he is right. "But we really are romantic," observes Cliff.

As I prepared for the long journey, researcher Tee Snell emerged from the Library of Congress in Washington, D. C., her arms loaded with notes, maps, and sketches. Reliable highway information was often as hard to find as the route of 11th-century Turkoman cavalry across Persia and Asia Minor. But Tee found both. We would soon be ready—except for a photographer.

And then, out of the African bush, came word from National Geographic photographer Bruce Dale. He could join us in midsummer.

"And meantime why don't you and Cliff Lee take a shakedown cruise?" Tee suggested. "You could attend the big Gypsy pilgrimage in May at Saintes Maries de la Mer, in southern France."

So it was that Cliff made his first trip outside the British Isles, and I began consorting with his "outlandysshe People."

Farrier removes a worn shoe from a horse at the Appleby Fair. A Gypsy charmer (left) stoops to plant a kiss on her dozing father.

*J*ogging along an ancient Roman road, a horse
seller shows off his steed at Appleby.
Roman conquerors, developing trade and
communications in England, encouraged horse
fairs and markets almost 2,000 years ago.
Most fairs surviving today date from the late
Middle Ages. In the 18th century, English poet
John Gay, perhaps with Gypsies in mind, sang
of the carnival atmosphere, of "Punch's feats,
of pockets picked in crowds, and various cheats."

*P*iebald pony waits patiently
outside an Appleby pub; a prospective buyer
haggles with the owner over the
gilded cart. At right, a Gypsy rider
clip-clops through busy traffic.
In the evening, after a day of horse
trading, men gather to quaff beer.

Stone causeway arches above the dappled Eden River, where riders cool and water their horses. The lot of English Gypsies, previously within the law only when on the move, has gradually improved. Passed in 1968, the Caravan Sites Act called for establishment of more campsites for the wandering folk.

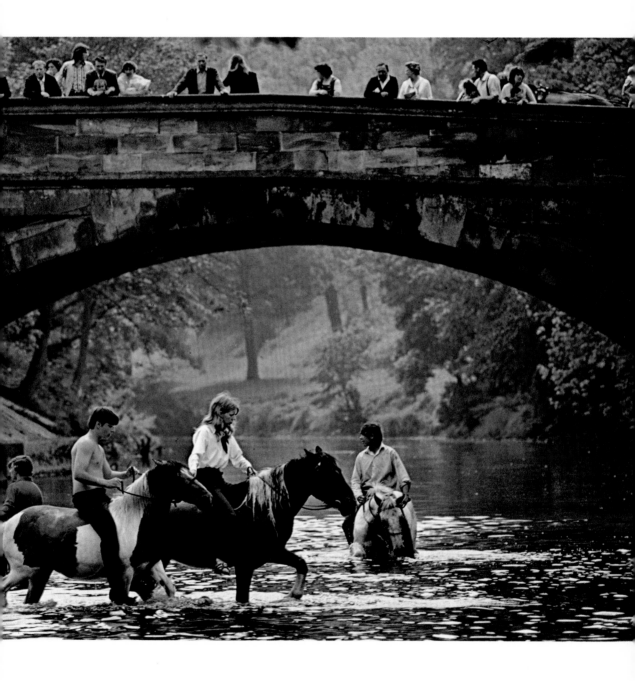

Carefully and lovingly decorated vardos, *or Gypsy caravans,*
often change hands along with horses at the Appleby Fair. A cut-glass
bouquet (above) sprouts in the window of a house trailer; a bright
sunflower blossoms on the door of a barrel-top caravan. As more Gypsies
settle down, vardos such as these become collectors' prizes.

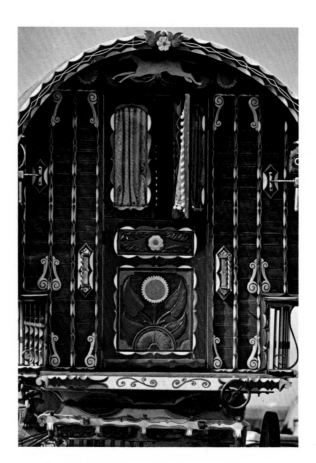

Darkness enfolds an encampment of Gypsies at Appleby. Their blazing fire, before a semicircle of caravans, lights a peaceful scene on Fair Hill; gossip and reminiscences end the day. Tomorrow the call of another road may tempt them onward.

Candles flicker in the crypt of Gypsy Saint Sarah the Black.

Pilgrimage to the Sea

OR HIS FIRST PLANE TRIP Cliff bought no flight insurance. "That's like putting the black mark on myself, like the evil eye or wishing myself dead," he said in honest horror. But after his nerves calmed he took an interest in the French countryside below us; then he grew wistful: "This will be the first night I've spent away from Sheila since we were wed 24 years ago. That's the way with Gypsies, you know. We travel, but the whole family goes together."

Cliff had history with him. In such family fashion the first Gypsies arrived on the outskirts of Paris in 1427. A witness described the "common herd ... they were not more in all, men, women, and children, than about

38

a hundred or a hundred and twenty.... their children, boys and girls, were as clever as could be; all had both ears pierced, and a silver ring or two in each.... The women were the ugliest that could be seen and the blackest; all had hair as black as a horse's tail.... In short, they were the poorest creatures ever seen coming to France within the memory of man; and in spite of their poverty there were witches in this company who looked into people's hands and told what had happened to them, or would happen."

They claimed to be "Christians...of Lower Egypt" who had "surrendered to their enemies and become Saracens as before, and denied Our Lord," and then been given a papal penance to "roam the earth for seven years without sleeping in a bed."

Yet their behavior seemed impious. As our witness recorded, "They sowed discord in several marriages by telling... the wife, 'your husband has deceived you.' And what was worse ... with the help of the enemy in hell or by their dexterity, they emptied people's purses and put them into their own.... The news came to the Bishop of Paris who went there ... excommunicating all those who had told fortunes together with all who had believed them.... And in the end they had to go away...."

Soon after landing in Paris, we too had to leave, flying on south to the feast of Sarah, the Gypsies' saint, at the town of Saintes Maries de la Mer, on the Île de la Camargue at the mouth of the Rhône River.

As we arrived, flashy motor cars were pulling fleets of trailers through the streets. *"Romanichals!* — Romanies!" said Cliff with obvious satisfaction. On the deep beaches beyond the seawall, and in high flat fields, Gypsies were beginning to pitch camp. Already the town seemed noisy. Naked children squealed. Mustachioed men shouted greetings. Women, some in the ruffled skirts of southern Spain and others in the earth-sweeping swirls of Hungary, gossiped and laughed. A number strung clotheslines in the white sunshine; others strolled through the cobbled streets with loaves of dark bread tucked under their arms. Everywhere radios blared with a volume just below the threshold of pain.

"Hey! Over here!" someone shouted, and at a sidewalk cafe I saw old friend Albert Moldvay, his cameras dangling like necklaces. A Geographic colleague, Al could spare time between assignments to help out until Bruce Dale joined us in Britain. "And here are other people who can help," said Al. He therewith presented two companions, Monique, a properly bespectacled young French interpreter, and María, an utterly improper Gypsy hag. I extended my hand.

"Tu suerte! Your fortune!" shrieked María in Spanish, turning my palm upward. I pulled back. But María, her voice like a gravel pit, kept up the hardest sell in Saintes Maries. She moved close and put her witch face close to mine, radiating a scent of black tobacco and yellow *pastis,* that anise-flavored inebriant of the south of France. So I bought a fortune to get some fresh air.

María switched to French for my rosy, banal fortune, then tried to sell me a religious medal. The very idea seemed scandalous. María's personal blessing could guarantee even a saint perdition. But I purchased her medal anyway — as a souvenir.

Cliff was disappointed in me and even more disappointed in María ("poor besotted soul"). Suddenly María turned her charms on him.

"*Your* fortune!" she rasped, and caught Cliff's arm in her claws. He struggled. "*Mandi Angitrako Rom!*" he said. "I'm an English Gypsy!" Finally María recognized the union rules, let Cliff off, and left — "mumbling a black mass in heaven knows what language," Cliff guessed.

We promptly upgraded the quality of our associates, looking up the Reverend Father Jean Fleury. A longtime authority on Romanies, Father Fleury once served as Roman Catholic Chaplain of all French Gypsies. Beneath his beret, his round sunburned face had a puckish look.

"Would you care to see some of my Gypsy friends?" he asked. We strolled among the campsites, watching families arrive. A dark-eyed Romany woman in a black dress ran up to the priest, kissed his hand, and got him to bless a religious medal. Next we passed some *gendarmes* arguing heatedly in the street with two trailerfuls of Gypsies.

"You are illegally parked here!" the gendarmes shouted. "Move on!"

When the officers left, Father Fleury advised the Gypsies, "The gendarmes are reasonable men — and also quite busy. Surely they will not return soon. And parking is not a sin." At once the grateful Gypsies began to unfurl an awning, make a charcoal fire, and settle in.

"You were in the Resistance during World War II," I remarked. "And I see you wear the red ribbon of the Legion of Honor."

"Yes. I began my study of Gypsies then, in 1942 at the concentration camp near Poitiers." So Father Fleury discussed the period of history when France's Vichy regime delivered both Jews and Gypsies to the Nazi occupation. "The local rabbi was not allowed to go into the camp, so I carried messages between him and the Jews and between the Jews and their families. Actually I was forbidden to enter the Jewish compound too, but I was allowed to go into the adjoining Gypsy camp. So I visited the Gypsies — and they got me through their fence to see the Jews. Then, if the Gypsies saw the Germans approaching, they would warn me to return to their camp." And if the Nazis had found him? "The death penalty." And how many times had he slipped in? Father Fleury paused, thought, and said, "Perhaps 200 times."

"Didn't the guards ever inspect the fence in the Gypsy camp?" I asked.

Father Fleury laughed, and his blue eyes disappeared entirely. "Inspect?" he roared. "During all the war years, the Germans never once set foot in the Gypsy camp. They feared catching lice, or some disease!"

SOON we had reached the great stone church, which towers above the tile roofs of Saintes Maries. Built in the 12th century, it served as a fortress in the Middle Ages; today, as Professor Starkie says, it resembles "the empty hold of an ancient galleon." Visitors were beginning to crowd the Romanesque nave and to file down below the altar to the crypt of *Sara-la-Kali,* or Sarah the Black.

"The first time I've been inside a church for years," Cliff whispered as soon as Father Fleury left us. Two big-eyed Gypsy toddlers approached Cliff, their hands outstretched to beg. "No, *there's* the gorgio," Cliff laughed, pointing at me. But the youngsters were not convinced.

"It's your gold rings," I said. "Anyone can tell you're the rich one." Cliff makes but two concessions to the fashion of his people: a silk scarf, and heavy gold rings on each hand.

By tradition, this feast celebrates a legendary event in A.D. 42, when two Biblical relatives, or "sisters," of the Virgin Mary, Saint Mary Jacobe, and Saint Mary Salome, mother of the Saints John and James, landed on this shore. The story tells that they drifted here in a small boat without oars or sails all the way from the Holy Land. With them came the swarthy Egyptian servant girl Sarah, considered by the Gypsies as their patron saint. And it is Sarah that they come to honor each May 24 and 25.

We pushed past the throngs, ducked our heads, and descended to the crypt, where Cliff gasped out, "It's the fiery furnace!" So it seemed. An English television crew, there to film the event, had filled the low, arched vault with powerful lights. In addition Gypsies had lighted hundreds of candles. The place pulsed with heat. And now the long tallow tapers had begun to melt, writhing into limp, surrealistic shapes and liquefying into waxy pools. In the molten center stood the three-foot-tall plaster figure of Saint Sarah, festively gowned, crowned, and as dark as any of her admirers. For a few moments we watched the faithful kiss her clothing and her face as they filed past. Gypsies would keep a vigil here for two days during the feast.

"Let's take an oxygen break," said Cliff. We stepped over coiled television cables and lakes of tallow, and emerged into the nave.

"Sorry about the heat," said one of the television men.

"Do you leave all this equipment unguarded?" Cliff asked in disbelief. "Is it safe?"

"Nothing stolen yet," said the technician.

Cliff shook his head dubiously. "Maybe all the bad ones stay near the bar. It's almost like two different peoples," Cliff mused. "See how the pious ones have parked their caravans here near the church. And they wear conservative clothes. Down by the waterfront it's entirely different. Loud music. Women with ruffled skirts." Cliff paused. "Perhaps we should see what's going on down there." And so we commuted between the sacred and the profane.

The street in front of the City Hall seethed with animation. "More Gypsies than I've ever seen together before," marveled Cliff.

"Your fortune!" grated a familiar voice, now in French. On a wave of prosperity, the unsteady María had forgotten the present as well as our future. We fended her off. Switching to Spanish, she muttered, "*Sí, sí. Gitano inglés* —English Gypsy," and teetered away.

By now kiosks had sprouted along the sidewalks. Roulette wheels whirred. Patrons stood 20-deep at the bars. And in the open arcade individual clusters of Gypsies were forming around guitar players.

With Cliff I pushed to the edge of the largest crowd, and found myself beside a lean, dark Gypsy wearing a flat Andalusian hat. I wondered who was playing, so I asked, "*¿Quién está tocando?*"

"Manitas de Plata," my neighbor answered. Manitas de Plata (literally, "Little Hands of Silver" in Spanish) is a world-famous flamenco guitarist. An illiterate Gypsy, he signs his name by first drawing a guitar, then

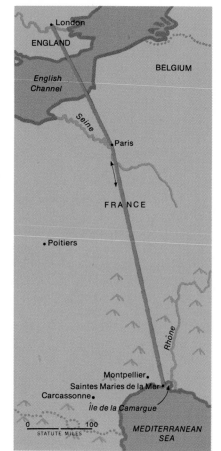

Author McDowell's Gypsy hunt includes a pilgrimage to Saintes Maries de la Mer in the south of France. There Romanies gather every May to honor the legend of Sarah, a servant girl they consider their patron saint.

41

laboriously adding the word "Manitas." "We Gypsies are very proud of Manitas," my companion said, lowering his dark eyes. "My name is Pepe Jiménez. You perhaps have heard of Manitas?"

Pepe was pleased that I knew even the artist's real name, Ricardo Ballardo, and that I had heard his records.

Manitas comes, I learned, not from Spanish Andalusia but from a Spanish Gypsy family living in Montpellier, only 30 miles from Saintes Maries. "Yes, we are more Spanish than the Gypsies of Granada," Pepe said. "Many of us came to France in the 1930's—during the Spanish civil war."

Applause drowned our words for a moment, and I turned to find Cliff.

"An English Gypsy?" Pepe exclaimed when I introduced them. "The same blood!" Cliff tried to hide his surprise and his British reserve as Pepe suddenly seized him in a hearty embrace, but he had begun to thaw. We adjourned to the cafe for an aperitif and a visit. Pepe and Cliff gestured their way through a language litany.

"Nak," said Cliff, pointing to his nose, "dand, bal, mui." In turn, he pointed to his teeth, hair, and face.

Pepe, a native of Barcelona, responded with similar Spanish-Gypsy equivalents: naki, dani, bal, mui.

When the index finger failed, Cliff used me as his Spanish translator: "Tell him we call a horse a grai, a dog a jakel. . . ."

Over glasses of cloudy pastis the talk turned serious as Pepe recalled the old days. "Yes, begged bread tasted the best . . . and food seasoned with hunger. My parents told me, 'You can beg—why do you need to go to school?' And so I was still illiterate at 13. I taught myself to read. Now I have two children going to school in Paris."

That night we ate an unbegged dinner together, and next day Pepe introduced us to his uncle Félix Cargolés, an obviously prosperous entrepreneur from Carcassonne. Félix fixed Cliff with a shrewd eye and, determined to impress the Anglo-Romany, pulled us to his long, sparkling trailer for a visit. His brand-new Mercedes-Benz, his chinaware, the plastic flowers brimming from bright vases, his chromium-trimmed table—everything added up to what Cliff called "a good flash," something instantly impressive.

"I cannot read or write," Félix announced. "But I have eight employees." And this Gypsy's line of work? "I am a used-car dealer."

As PART of the religious program Friday evening, we paraded through town in a procession. Our fellow pilgrims, the pious Gypsies, all carried lighted tapers as we moved down the gentle slope, past caravans parked on the beach, and along honky-tonk row. Here we saw some of our fun-loving friends; they stopped the roulette wheels as we passed, but they seemed a bit embarrassed for us—and a little distrustful when we saw them next. Then on Saturday I joined Father Fleury with some of his faithful Gypsies for a glass of wine. Several gendarmes approached our table.

"You did us a disservice, Father," said one policeman coldly. "You told the Gypsies they could continue to park in an illegal zone."

Father Fleury tried to mollify the police, but the quarrel warmed up. Other officers joined in and began to question some Gypsies standing nearby. I wasn't able to follow the impassioned French, but the gestures

Television antenna sprouts from the hitch of a Gypsy trailer. This band of Hungarians — beggars and fortune-tellers — camps at Saintes Maries de la Mer from February to May despite a law requiring them to move on after 48 hours. To circumvent it, says the mayor, "they stay two days, leave for one day, and return for another two days."

were theatrical, and I couldn't resist this age-old rivalry of law-versus-Gypsy. I took out my camera and, to get pictures of the gendarmes' expressive faces, leaned and squatted and stooped. Then, quite suddenly, I heard the voice of authority directed at me.

"You! Yes, you," said the officer angrily. "Give me your camera."

I could understand his imperatives but couldn't really speak his language, so I hailed Monique to act as my mouthpiece. "Tell him no," I instructed her. "Isn't this a public place?"

"Yes," said the gendarme, as he took me by the arm. "But I am not a national monument. It is not necessary to stoop down in such fashion to take my picture. Let me see your passport."

I didn't have it with me. Suddenly, I felt as illegal as any trespassing Gypsy. With grave suspicion, he began escorting me across the street for uninterrupted questioning. "You can accompany me to my hotel," I said. "My passport is there."

"No, you go at once and bring it to me here," he ordered. From the corner of my eye, I could see Gypsies gathering; elbows prodded neighbors; a silence fell, and I sensed a certain sympathy from the crowd.

Monique seemed very nervous. "Tell him if I go, I refuse to return,"

43

I said with fever rising. "Or he can arrest me now and take me to jail."

Monique gasped, blushed, and would not translate. So I tried on my own. My angry French must have been vivid—and truly terrible. Everyone within earshot began to laugh. Even my hardhearted captor broke out laughing. He released me forthwith, then offered his outstretched hand. We shook. The crowd dissolved.

In the excitement everyone had forgotten the illegally parked Gypsies. But they had not forgotten me. Thereafter, Gypsies I'd never met hailed me on the street as a brother outlaw. They even bought me drinks and offered me black cigarettes.

So I sat at a sidewalk table and jotted all sorts of overheard comments into my notebook. I did not, however, write anything down in the presence of the Gypsies. They grow nervous at the sight of a notebook—for fear it's a police citation.

Consider these exact, unattributed stories, told only partly in jest:

"The best way to steal a chicken is to use a horsewhip. From a distance, you can flick the whip and wrap it around the neck of the hen. She can't even squawk. But if noise is no problem, one can tie a string to a grain of corn and let the hen swallow it. Then—*voilà!*—you pull the hen off by a string attached to its gizzard."

"For selling an old horse, you can pick out the natural hollows in the crowns of the teeth and fill them with tar to look like the black centers of a young horse's teeth. They will fool even an experienced trader."

Cliff laughed indulgently at such tricks, but not wholeheartedly. He was like a man who chuckles over boyish Halloween pranks—until someone plays them on him. "Remember that a Gypsy might lift a chicken and never dream of robbing a farmer's house," he said loyally.

We also collected material from the less mischievous pilgrims.

"I met some Italian Gypsies of the Sinti tribe today," said Cliff. "Their Romany is more like ours than that of the French and Spanish Gypsies. And their ways. They were peddlers of china and ivory."

"Now there's a man with an earring," said Cliff. "Just one in the left ear. In England you could be sure he was a fake Gypsy, usually a sailor, and he'd tell you he wears an earring to improve his eyesight. But in France, a real Gypsy wears one to mark him as a leader."

THE CITY HALL stood across the street from the sidewalk cafe, so I had to slip in to see the mayor. He was, after all, a *muskro*, a term Cliff applies to all officials from generals to game wardens.

"Welcome!" said Mayor Roger Delagnes. His Excellency also serves in the French Senate in Paris, and his gray Louis XIV desk itself resembles a branch of the government. "You are interested in our statistics. *Bon.* Our year-round village residents number 2,300. We have 50,000 people in the summer. And yesterday we had 80,000." And how was this count taken? "We know from the amount of bread we bake daily. Allowing five persons to the kilo, we can project the figures with great logic. And we estimate that of the 80,000 people, 8,000 were Gypsies.

"We have special problems. Today we have twice our summertime force, 50 gendarmes to direct traffic and 12 more specialists in controlling *mauvais garçons*—bad boys—some Gypsies, some hippies."

"We have already met some of your specialists," I admitted.

"To prevent fortune-telling we would need one gendarme per Gypsy," His Excellency shrugged. "But we have both good and bad Gypsies.

"Of course, our village has no year-round Gypsy population. Gypsies can only stay in one place two days at a time, then they must move. This doesn't hold true during the pilgrimage, when they can remain ten days.

"But—*regardez*—we have about four families of Hungarian Gypsies who stay from February to May. Certainly we cannot banish them by force. They stay two days, leave for one day, and return for another two days. They beg and tell fortunes and bother our visitors. I would give a pretty penny to get rid of those disagreeable guests!

"And yet," the Mayor sighed deeply, "I realize that it is thanks to the Gypsies that our village is famous."

With more questions, I called on Father André Barthélémy, successor to Father Fleury as Catholic Chaplain of the French Gypsies. "Actually this is the oldest pilgrimage in France. Not as a Gypsy feast, of course. Gypsies began coming in the 19th century," said the Father. "Only about 30 or 40 families at first. But do not misunderstand. The cult of Sarah is only folklore. Sarah is not a saint of the Church.

BART McDOWELL, NATIONAL GEOGRAPHIC STAFF

"Gypsies have always gone their own way. They have a unity because of society's opposition. If people accepted Gypsies, they would cease to exist as a separate group.

"This year we have a new law concerning wanderers in France. You have seen the old carnet?" I had. The carnet, a kind of internal passport for rovers, used to require fingerprints and pages of detailed personal information, even chest measurements. "Well, a carnet is still required, though perhaps it permits more dignity. And the new laws are more positive, attempting to educate Gypsy children. You know, we have an estimated 100,000 Gypsies in France; 25,000 of them still roam. Perhaps the new laws will bring the Gypsies more respect. But," Father Barthélémy smiled, "I hope they won't cease to be Gypsies. For then we should have to invent them."

No inventions were necessary just yet. In an ocean of human bodies we watched Gypsies on Sunday afternoon bring the image of Sarah up from her candle-heated crypt. The little figure bobbed and trembled as her bearers placed her before the altar. Delegations of dressed-up Gypsies—tides of sequins, plumes, and ruffles—carried in bouquets of flowers that wilted almost instantly in the hot church.

Gallic gestures punctuate a dispute over Gypsy parking rights. The author faced arrest after taking this picture, but his fractured French turned wrath to mirth.

Now the congregation was singing a treacly hymn. A child cried. A baby cooed. And I heard Cliff ask a neighbor, "Is it true you still eat hedgehog in Spain?"

We craned our necks toward the ceiling. From an opening in the stone wall high above the altar three men began to lower two coffin-shaped reliquaries. These boxes, the faithful believe, contain relics of *les Saintes Maries,* so a momentary stillness fell over the crowd. A choirmaster started new hymns as the coffins slowly descended, trailing ropes entwined with garlands of flowers. The hymn trickled to a close; the crowd buzzed with anticipation. And now the fortress-church shook with a full-throated shout as big as a cannon volley:

"Vivent les Saintes Maries!"

N.G.S. PHOTOGRAPHER ALBERT MOLDVAY

Then from the Gypsies sounded a smaller but no less intense salute: *"Vive la Sainte Sarah!"*

Dignity turned into a religious free-for-all. Members of the choir stood on tiptoe, holding their candles high, thrusting them toward the base of the descending coffins. "It's good luck," said a woman beside me, "to snuff the flame against the bottom of the box."

Later that evening a cold west wind blew up, ventilating the cafes and bringing a film of thin, gray clouds. Al Moldvay, eager for pictures, studied the sky with ill humor. But the British television cameraman had far lower morale.

"A lens," he said. "It was taken right off the camera. Vanished."

"What could he expect?" shrugged a woman kiosk-keeper. "With 8,000 Gypsies in town."

"And 72,000 gorgios," muttered Cliff.

I was amazed, myself, that more things had not disappeared. For days a whole photo bazaar had lain open: cameras, lights, film clips, coils of electric cord—everything quite vulnerable and unguarded. Now one lens was gone. One thief out of 80,000 people.

All of them—Gypsy and gorgio, pious and profane—assembled now for the last great event: the annual procession to the sea. In the crowded courtyard beside the church the Gypsies seemed diluted by French tourists. A parade formed noisily to the clopping sound of hoofs on cobblestones. The riders were the *gardians,* or Camargue cowboys, mounted on strong white cowponies with stumpy, functional saddles.

We reached the sandy shore in a carnival atmosphere. Only the bearers of the images retained a spirit of piety. I watched, my feet awash in the tide, as they dipped the statues three times into the Mediterranean.

Sheepishly, hoping none of my pious friends would notice, I took a deck of tarot cards from my pocket and dunked them briefly into the sea. "Excellent for fortune-telling," one Gypsy had told me. "But be quick—the cards must touch the sea while the saints are still there."

I slipped the cards back into my pocket, wet and sticky with salt. And then we returned to the village.

But it was immediately apparent that something was amiss. Even as gorgios spread picnic meals, I could see Gypsy caravans on the move, outbound. Around the campsites, litter and cold ashes showed spots where families had already left.

"It's all over—you can feel it," said Cliff when I met him again. "Only the gorgios are staying—for the bullfights and the rodeo." But he was only part right. Scandalous old María appeared with bleary eye and outstretched palm. "No, no," said Cliff. *"Rom anglais!* English Gypsy!"

She continued anyway: "Just a few francs," she whined, "for food."

"For pastis, you mean," Cliff accused. "María, you should give *me* money," he teased. She paused and blinked at Cliff. *"Tacho rat*—for the true blood?" he added. Taken aback, the unsteady hag reached deep into a pocket and pulled out a handful of bills. Wordlessly, and with an indifferent shrug, she presented them to Cliff.

"Dearie *Devel!*" he said. "She means it. Thank you, *puri bibi*—old aunt—but I was only joking."

So we bought María a drink for fond farewell. "Which is probably what she had in mind all along," said Cliff gruffly.

*D*ecor of
gaudy opulence frames
a Hungarian Gypsy
mother and child
in their caravan home.

"Vivent les Saintes Maries!" *cry worshipers as reliquaries*

descend on garlanded ropes from a small chapel high in the church of Notre

Dame de la Mer. The caskets contain relics venerated as those

of the Biblical sisters of the Virgin Mary — Mary Jacobe and Mary Salome.

Pilgrims strain to snuff their candles on the boxes, thereby assuring

themselves of good luck. Soon the Gypsies will shout their own salute,

"Vive la Sainte Sarah!" in honor of the servant girl who legend

says served the two Saints Mary. Above, a priest baptizes a Gypsy infant.

In the stifling, smoky crypt of the church, Gypsy men, women, and children pay homage to Sarah. Natural performers and intense spectators, they create a spontaneous religious drama with an impromptu concert. As fervor rises, roles change: Spectators become performers. Candles melt in the heat, and incense fumes mingle with the smoke, but the faithful will ignore discomforts and keep their vigil.

$\mathcal{B}$orne aloft through the town, the Saints symbolically
return to the sea that legend says cast them up in a small
boat nearly 2,000 years ago. Celebrants—some of them mounted
Camargue cowboys—follow the procession into the Mediterranean
and cheer as bearers immerse the figures three times.

Sacred and secular coexist at Saintes Maries.

As the devout throng the church, revelers perform rites of their own.

The group below, part of the street dancing

and sidewalk singing the photographer found, improvises a concert.

Ricardo Ballardo (left), world-famous flamenco guitarist,

uses the stage name Manitas de Plata — "Little Hands of Silver."

N.G.S. PHOTOGRAPHER ALBERT MOLDVAY (ABOVE) AND BART McDOWELL, N.G.S. STAFF

*asket weaver (below) plies his craft for
the tourist trade at Saintes Maries de la Mer. Stoic courage
in an old man's eyes (opposite) recalls a Gypsy philosophy
recorded by an English writer: "Always help brothers;
never harm brothers; always pay when you owe
although not necessarily money; and never be afraid."*

NATIONAL GEOGRAPHIC PHOTOGRAPHER GEORGE F. MOBLEY

Author McDowell and the Lees share the first meal of the trip, a picnic on the River Thames.

Gypsy Violins, Nazi Death Camps

AFTER YEARS OF DAYDREAMING and months of planning, Sheila, Cliff, Bruce, and I began our journey on a July day picnicking beside the River Thames. This was our first meal together, for we'd converged from all directions. With difficulty, we had fitted all our luggage — even Sheila's sewing machine — into a single car, the Land-Rover camper. Now we sprawled on the grass, studying the highway maps.

"You noticed the road sign back there?" Cliff asked me. I had not. "Well, it said Runnymede." He waited for the drama to penetrate: We were beginning our journey beside the same "meadow called Ronimed between Windsor and Staines" where King John signed the Magna Carta in 1215. Among the freedoms he guaranteed was the one "for anyone to leave our kingdom, and to return, safe and sound, by land and by water. . . ." Now we would exercise that special freedom over a 13,000-mile trail, east and south, "traveling as free as Gypsies," said Cliff.

We followed the Thames as it broadened, crossed it at Kew, and bypassed London. Like Chaucer's pilgrims, we saw the noble spires of Canterbury, then flocks of sheep and ripening Kentish fields of wheat.

We reached Dover in the amber sun of late afternoon, and drove onto the Channel ferry. Now I had time to scribble in my notebook:

"We watch towering chalky cliffs recede as sun sets. Squawling squadrons of gulls roil the red sky. Eat in ferryboat dining room. I ask, does Cliff consider himself an English or a Welsh Gypsy? He says, 'Just a Gypsy—a cat that's born on a pillow isn't a cat-a-pillow.' "

But over dinner, as dusk fell on the Channel, our talk took a darker turn. We spoke of Adolf Hitler's efforts to cross this water and of his Gypsy persecutions. The dark mood held as we disembarked at Calais by night. Not yet equipped for camping, we found depressing rooms in a small hotel, and there, by the light of a bare electric bulb, I read my notes about an earlier visit with Mateo Maximoff in Paris.

Picture a bland, round-faced man of middle age. He looks at the world through eyes pale and bespectacled—yet aglow with a fierce intensity. This is Mateo Maximoff, an ordained minister of the Gypsy Evangelical Church and perhaps the world's only Gypsy novelist. (If he is untypical of the estimated 100,000 Gypsies in France, his church nonetheless claims 30,000 French members.) He belongs to the Kalderash, or coppersmith, Gypsies—one of the tribes from eastern Europe that took part in a revival of international wandering in the late 19th century. Mateo talks slowly, cadencing his speech like an incantation:

"My family? *Bon.* My mother was a French Gypsy, a tightrope walker. She died when I was 8. Father was a Russian Gypsy, and he died when I was 14. I had five younger brothers and sisters, so I served as the head of the family until everyone was old enough to marry. We lived everywhere—France, Germany, Holland, Norway, Finland—in all, 15 countries.

"We were in France in 1938, in the Province of Auvergne, when we Gypsies had a private war among ourselves. A duel of honor. It concerned a girl, my first cousin, deserted by her husband. Family quarrels, oaths. Then a three-minute battle with shotguns, knives, and stones. Three died: two on our side—my uncle and aunt—and one of the others. Perhaps, on both sides, 20 were wounded.

"Well, the French authorities impartially ordered all Gypsy males over 15 arrested. I was 21, so I went to jail, and what good fortune it was! While in prison, I wrote a novel in 31 days, and I gave it to my lawyer, Jacques Isorni. Yes, I was literate; my father had taught me to read.

"Time passed. The war came, and the German occupation. The Nazis organized 11 concentration camps inside France just for Gypsies. I was a prisoner for more than three years in two camps in the Pyrenees. One, called Gurs, was an old 1914 hospital with its doors and windows missing. We put only cloth over the openings, even when we had deep snow and sub-zero temperatures. I owned but one jacket for all those years.

"Many of us died. To earn one bowl of soup we had to gather a truck-load of wood. I have seen a Gypsy carry out the garbage, and then fight other prisoners with his pocketknife for a rotting fish head.

"We were permitted to leave the camp and work in town ten days each month. If we returned late we were fined two days' pay.

"I weighed 75 kilos when I entered Gurs. In two years I weighed but 44 kilos—just 97 pounds.

"Then I got word from the lawyer. My novel had been printed. I received 6,000 francs—an unheard-of treasure when I was making only

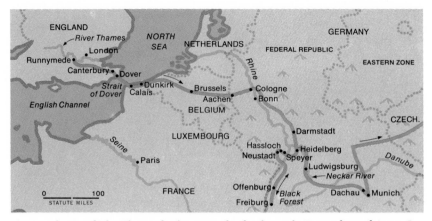

Across the English Channel, the route leads through Brussels and into Germany, where Gypsy musicians recall the horrors of Nazi concentration camps.

43 francs a day. Somehow I survived the camps to write four other novels. And to preach the Gospel here."

Mateo Maximoff, Gypsy-of-letters, adds a note that may explain his vocation. "In the concentration camps I learned how awful men can be. And yet, our camps were not as bad as those in Germany."

Toward the scenes of those Gypsy persecutions we now made our way. From Calais we drove along the coast, pausing for lunch on a beach near Dunkirk. Cliff, munching on hard French bread, reminisced:

"Our family had been traveling in Ireland for years by the time the war came. Many a Gypsy served in the British army. Before, in the first World War, I had three uncles killed. My poor grandmother. She never ate an orange or cooked a Christmas pudding after that war. One of her dead sons had loved oranges and puddings. Nor did she mention his name, of course." Cliff didn't mention the name either.

We crossed the Belgian border, and sped past canals where yellow-haired youngsters sat fishing. Draft horses, bulky as elephants, pulled wagonloads of cargo, and placid milk cows stood tall upon the flat horizon. We passed sandy resorts and vacationists with light hearts and heavy luggage racks.

In Brussels we met Antoine Demol, a reporter for the newspaper *Het Laatste Nieuws* — The Latest News — who knows all the 60 families of Belgian Gypsies. "Yes, I write letters for them and visit them in the hospital and in jail. I am, unofficially, the ambassador of the Gypsies."

With Antoine one night we proceeded to a rowdy part of the city where bright lights blinked invitations to shooting galleries, tattoo parlors, and merry-go-rounds.

"The Fair of Brussels," Antoine noted. "A tradition for 100 years. These Gypsies follow the carnivals." We spent an evening with the carnival Gypsies in a beer hall called the Tête de Veau — Calf's Head.

But our evening was under a pall. One boy named Modeste had recently shot two of his cousins. A feud was boiling between the two families, and the cousins' partisans were demanding blood money.

Everyone was moody, but not, I felt, simply because of the fight. I could feel a wariness — almost a distrust — of the outsider. There was a quiet, thin woman named Medela. She looked strongly Gypsy with that quicksilver quality. She seemed uncomfortable, and left early. Antoine whispered an explanation: "She had two children. Her son was 17 when the Nazis caught him in Paris. Killed in Buchenwald. Then her daughter was caught and also killed."

And to her Bruce and I were gorgios—as were the Nazi troopers.

In a slow rain that Cliff found "just like Liverpool," we drove on toward the German border. After we cleared customs, Bruce eased the Land-Rover onto the broad autobahn. A sign announced Aachen, reminding me of a fierce battle in World War II—and of something else that happened there. I leafed through my research papers and found that Gypsiologist Martin Block had recorded the following local law, dated 1728:

"...in order to root out this brood of rascals...whether the Gypsies resist or not, these people shall be put to death. Nevertheless, those who ...do not counterattack may be granted at most half an hour, to go on their knees and beg of the Almighty, if they so wish, pardon for their sins and to prepare for death...."

Yet in the beginning the Gypsies had known a golden age in Germany as well as in other countries of western Europe, while they were still accepted as pilgrims. In the early 15th century German peasants generously gave them gifts and permission to camp near their villages.

"Then, most likely, we wore out our welcome," said Cliff.

In an account of the "miserable state of these people," the scholar Grellmann agreed. "They were not always even looked upon as human creatures, for at a hunting party, at one of the small German courts, a mother and her sucking child, were shot like a couple of wild beasts."

AT COLOGNE, Bruce and I acquired a Volkswagen Camper, repacked both cars, and—at last equipped to pitch a proper camp—moved on. We passed Darmstadt, seat of the former grand duchy of Hesse-Darmstadt. A story by French writer Jean-Paul Clébert says that here in the mid-18th century a Gypsy band camped with one vagabond violinist so brilliant that the mayor offered him the job of town choirmaster. The musician, it happened, was not a Gypsy at all but Wilhelm Friedemann Bach, eldest son of Johann Sebastian Bach. After much correspondence Wilhelm accepted the Darmstadt title, but not the position.

"So, you see, the story had a happy ending," said Cliff. It did. Bach was still free to wander with the Gypsies, who, according to both fact and legend, had encouraged and influenced him as a young artist.

Just down the road, in Heidelberg, we too joined some Gypsy musicians, the Schnuckenack Reinhardt Quintet.

"It's a good Gypsy name," said Schnuckenack when we met him. "In our Romany, *shukar nak* means 'pretty-nose.'" He turned a profile to show his noble nak. Though he acts the role of the playful fat man, Schnuckenack is the most famous Gypsy violinist in Germany.

"Now meet the others," said Siegfried Maeker, manager of the quintet. "Daweli Reinhardt, solo guitar; Spatzo Weiss, rhythm guitar; and Hojok Merstein, bass. The group is short a rhythm guitar until tomorrow."

We were meeting in Maeker's Heidelberg apartment over a Sunday feast. Maeker, a young lawyer of Russian background, got caught up in Gypsy music during his university days in Bonn. Now he speaks fluent

Romany and — far harder — keeps the schedule for this mercurial quintet. "We're here to record an album tomorrow," Maeker explained.

Over liverwurst and mugs of beer, we talked. "Don't take notes," Maeker cautioned. "Even after all these years they are still fearful. Many of the people in this room have been imprisoned in concentration camps. They live near the French border: In case of trouble they could move quickly.... You want to hear their music?" We did.

"But it's Gypsy jazz!" Bruce exclaimed. And it was: Schnuckenack's fiddle carried a touch of Liszt and "Satchmo." We then heard old Gypsy tunes — the raucous *"Me Ham Matto,"* meaning "I am Drunk" in Romany, and *"Fuli Tschai,"* or "Bad Girl."

"That's a nice translation," said Cliff. "Gypsies speak in oral graffiti." As the music romped on, Maeker told us how the Sinti style began long ago with Gypsy folk songs and a Hungarian flavor. In recent years Django Reinhardt, the great Gypsy guitarist until his death in 1953, added a swing and jazz touch so distinctive it even influenced American music.

"Now Schnuckenack, another member of the wide-ranging Reinhardt clan, comes along," said Maeker. "During the Nazi persecutions, he learned the styles of other Gypsies in Europe — the Hungarian violin techniques, the Rumanian quarter tones — and he combined what he wanted. The concentration camps were like musical finishing schools — for those who survived."

URING THE REHEARSALS, we got better acquainted. Yet I could tell that Cliff was depressed. "I wish I knew more formal Romany grammar. Maybe I could understand them better," he said. From Maeker I got the same reaction: Except for isolated words, neither he nor the Gypsies could understand Cliff. "One of our Gypsies is afraid of Cliff, thinks he might be some kind of government spy. But not Schnuckenack. He invites you to the recording session tomorrow."

The studio was a cavern of acoustic tile, littered with coffee cups and serpentines of recording tape, and heavy with the odor of stale cigarettes.

"Where is Holzmanno?" asked Maeker. A young Gypsy boy stepped up with a guitar case. "Our new man," said Maeker. "Yesterday catching trout with his bare hands in the Black Forest, and today he records with our quintet."

"Trout?" asked Cliff, pantomiming an old Gypsy trick: tickling the fish gently on the throat and then lifting it out by the gills. Holzmanno Winterstein laughed nervously. He was only 17, and this was his big chance. He had stayed up all night rehearsing, and he had arrived late.

"Naturally," said Sheila gently. "The first eight years I was married, I didn't own a timepiece at all."

While the quintet worked, we went outside to wait on the banks of the Neckar River — and found two families of Gypsies camped there.

"Rom san?" I asked — "You are Gypsy?" They grinned, baffled that we knew Gypsy words. But when they saw us eating with Schnuckenack's group, we became easy friends. After they packed to go, the mother leaned out the window and called to Bruce: *"Amerikaner ist* Good Boy!"

Two days later we broke camp ourselves and headed south. We were traveling with Schnuckenack to take some of his musicians home — meaning wherever their families were camping. Along the Rhine Valley summer was swelling into the harvest season: Tobacco plants bloomed, grapes hung heavy on the vine, and apples were just blushing red.

We passed the city of Speyer on the banks of the Rhine, following close behind Schnuckenack's own car. He drives as he plays his fiddle: allegro, and with engaging ad libs. At the village of Hassloch we stopped.

"My house," said Schnuckenack proudly. "Built by myself." It sat behind a clover meadow, shaded by peach and plum trees, but Schnuckenack uses it only in winter.

Across the road a neighbor waved. "Good people," said Schnuckenack. "They sometimes bring us gifts—pheasants, rabbits, chickens."

We drove on, following our host's parabolic course all over the highway and, it seemed, all over Germany. Spatzo was camped at nearby Neustadt, and there, by chance, Schnuckenack's old father was visiting. I recalled the story Maeker had told us about this extraordinary family.

The Reinhardts—parents, three girls, three boys—were first imprisoned with other German Gypsies in the hilltop castle of Hohenasperg near Ludwigsburg. Then, in 1942, the whole family was put on a train bound for Poland. When the train stopped for track-switching at a small station one night, the father ordered his family off and into the darkness of Poland with only their violins and one guitar. They survived as free folk for two years, playing at peasant weddings, begging food, sleeping in barns, walking—always avoiding the highways. Near the end of the war, the Nazis caught them again. One of Schnuckenack's brothers died in prison, but the rest of the family survived.

"They were lucky," said Maeker. "No one knows how many Gypsies died in the persecution. Some say 600,000 from all countries under Nazi control, and I think this number could be correct. One thing we do know. Only an estimated 20,000 to 30,000 Gypsies live in Germany today."

Maeker always guarded against pronouncing certain names—like "Auschwitz" or "Dachau" or "Buchenwald" or "Hitler"—in front of the Gypsies. "It makes them suspicious," he said. The word *Hitlari*, in fact,

Gypsies treasure each moment as though it were gold: In a small Belgian cafe violins and trumpets play as rhythmic hands sound a beat that compels a dance.

NATIONAL GEOGRAPHIC PHOTOGRAPHER ALBERT MOLDVAY

is so hated that it has become a vile epithet among the German Sintis.

Gradually, though, confidence grew. I felt that Bruce and I had at last made the grade socially when Schnuckenack told Maeker: "I'm used to them. Find out if we can see them when we go on tour in the U.S.A." We exchanged telephone numbers, but not addresses, since the Gypsies could read only numerals.

We returned young Holzmanno to his father's camp near Offenburg, on the fringes of the Black Forest, a charming, poplar-shaded spot beside a canal. Nearby, as we toiled up a forested hill, we stopped again "to show you our favorite camping place among these hazelnut trees," said Schnuckenack. He disappeared for a moment, presumably to relieve himself — but no Gypsy would ever refer to such a matter.

"Strictly taboo to mention," said Cliff. "Our use of graffiti stops there. And do you know I never so much as saw Sheila change our children's nappies — diapers, as you say. She even washed them and hung them to dry out of my sight. Certain things are indelicate."

THE REINHARDTS were camped outside Freiburg, near the Swiss border. "We pay this farmer to camp in his pasture," Schnuckenack explained. He pointed happily to the wide field of deep grass, the splendid shade trees, and the cold, clear stream that gurgled in a rich contralto. "This is called Höllental — Hell's Valley," he laughed.

Schnuckenack's wife Kitta was seated on the grass mending eiderdown quilts. A large-eyed boy named Forello (Trout) was building a campfire. Sleek new cars and trailers made the camp luxurious. In my notebook I jotted down these words: *The cleanest campsite I have ever seen. Anywhere.* And it was infinitely more pleasant than the big, poorly maintained campgrounds at the edges of some cities where many settled Gypsies live on welfare, or the grounds near some towns where they can stay a night or two before the police move them on.

Mrs. Reinhardt is a handsome woman with a well-tanned skin and fine bright eyes. She moved energetically — but with effort for she was with child. "Her eighth," said Maeker. "And so far, the young Trout is the only boy." Trout grinned.

"Nights are cold here," said Kitta, "even after hot days. And the water is always cold." She marshaled children for the chores: grinding coffee beans, toasting bacon in the fire like marshmallows, fetching water from the stream, bringing pitchers of foamy milk fresh from the farmer's barn. As she worked, I noticed Kitta's left forearm.

"Is that a tattooed number?" I asked Maeker.

He nodded, then carefully spelled: "A-U-S-C-H-W-I-T-Z." It seemed a sickening incongruity in this wholesome setting. But Schnuckenack's wife had indeed been tattooed as a child in that dread concentration camp. So had her sister-in-law, a gray, crumpled woman who looked old enough to be her husband's mother. "She was married before," Maeker whispered. "Lost her family, five children, to the gas chambers." As darkness settled, she sat alone at the edge of the firelight.

Yet the melancholy mood soon dissolved in the warmth of the campfire. As the running stream played harmony, young Trout strummed a guitar for the pure fun of it. Just as naturally, his sisters danced barefoot on the cool grass — delightful, swirling, spontaneous motions. We watched until they grew bored and stopped. Then young Trout put himself to bed in the trailer, sprawled on his back with the guitar plopped upon his stomach. Relaxed, he strummed away. The tempo of his music slowed and finally merged with the deep, regular rhythm of his own breathing. Together, Trout and his guitar slept.

Our days with Schnuckenack's people put a spell on all of us. As we moved back northeast across Germany, we recalled places and events they had mentioned. At Ludwigsburg we climbed to the mountaintop castle of Hohenasperg, where the Reinhardts had been imprisoned, a dark stone fortress now used as a prison hospital. "What a terrible place for a Gypsy," Cliff said in a hushed voice. "A real *mulano* place — ghostly."

In March, 1933, a brief item appeared in the newspaper *Die Münchner Neuesten Nachrichten* — Munich's Latest News:

"On Wednesday . . . the first concentration camp will be opened in the vicinity of Dachau. . . . We have adopted this measure, undeterred by paltry scruples, in the conviction that our action will help to restore calm to our country and is in the best interests of our people."

This announcement, signed by Heinrich Himmler, established the first concentration camp of Hitler's Third Reich. The camp, nine miles northwest of Munich, operated for a full 12 years, until American troops liberated its prisoners in 1945. Here tens of thousands of men, women, and children died, and the site today stands as a memorial to those dead. Now, to document this part of Gypsy history, we journeyed to Dachau.

U.S.-made automobile attests the wealth of this used-car dealer, leader of a Belgian Gypsy tribe.

"The first Gypsy prisoners were brought here in 1938," said Mrs. Ruth Jakusch, director of the Dachau museum. "And today, Gypsy families still come to see the place where their relatives suffered. Some leave flowers. One family recently left two cigars and two bottles of beer, placed as a memorial. . . . But you should talk with a former prisoner here who remembers those first Gypsies."

So I drove to Munich for a visit with Otto Kohlhofer, now a government functionary in the agriculture department. Mr. Kohlhofer studies his visitors with intensely blue eyes; his face is etched by a net of deep lines.

"Yes, I remember those Gypsies," he said. "Jolly fellows. They came in the summer of 1938, mostly from Austria — about 2,000. They stayed together in the barracks numbered 20 to 30. I remember three Gypsy clans in particular: Horvath, Scharkösi, and Baranai. Most of them had a first name of Joseph. And in one room alone lived 50 named Joseph Horvath. Great confusion.

"Prison life was harder for the roamers than for the settled Gypsies. They were like wild birds. How could they understand confinement? They truly needed freedom. And they died first, I remember.

"All Gypsies wore the prison uniform — stripes, and a brown triangle upon the left breast and on their trousers. Yet they were allowed to bring their violins. Good: So that on Sundays they walked from building to

N.G.S. PHOTOGRAPHER ALBERT MOLDVAY

building, playing music for the other prisoners. One Jewish comedian from Austria joined them with an act. They cheered us up.

"In the winter of 1939-40, the Gypsies had to work very hard in the cold. Of the first 2,000, I know of none who lived."

In vain we looked for Gypsies camping near Dachau, though we ourselves found a "lovely gorgio campsite," as Sheila called it, within easy commuting distance of the Dachau museum and library. And there I read the stories of horror: medical experiments performed on the living... men killed and picked clean of their gold teeth ... people starved on food rations so small that one official of Hitler's dread Elite Guard, the SS, wrote, "An honest prisoner should not live longer than three months, otherwise he is a thief."

But worst of all, in the Dachau library I read the eerie autobiography of Rudolf Höss, commandant of the Auschwitz camp, where some 16,000 Gypsies were imprisoned. Höss claimed that as a small child "some traveling gypsies had found me playing by myself and had taken me away with them. I was rescued by a neighboring peasant...."

Perhaps. But Höss's later memories seem more reliable. Awaiting his own death sentence for war crimes, he wrote these observations:

"Long before the war gypsies were being rounded up ... as part of the campaign against asocials.... Although they were a source of great trouble to me at Auschwitz," Gypsies were "my best-loved prisoners—if I may put it that way.... They loved to play, even at work, which they never took quite seriously....

"I never saw a scowling, hateful expression on a gypsy's face. If one went into their camp, they would often ... play their musical instruments, or ... let their children dance.... When spoken to they would reply openly and trustingly....

"In July 1942 the Reichsführer SS [Heinrich Himmler] visited the ... gypsy camp.... He saw those who were sick ... and the children ... their little bodies wasted away ... a slow putrefaction of the living body.... He saw it all ... and he ordered me to destroy them.... About 4,000 gypsies were left by August 1944, and these had to go into the gas chambers. Up to that moment, they were unaware of what was in store for them. They first realized what was happening when they made their way, barrack hut by barrack hut toward crematorium I. It was not easy to drive them into the gas chambers.... Schwarzhuber [another camp official] told me that it was more difficult than any previous mass destruction of Jews, and it was particularly hard on him, because he knew almost every one of them individually....They were by their nature as trusting as children."

In the collection of wartime photographs, we saw emaciated Dachau prisoners tending the poplar saplings they had planted beside the Lagerstrasse, the central camp corridor. On our way to the library we passed the same trees—now 60 feet high and sighing in the wind. They served as living reminders of men who had planted them and perished.

"Even on a sunny day," said Cliff, "this place has a shadow over it."

On the day we left, he stood beneath a poplar and spat upon the earth, and with a grimness I never again saw on his face, Clifford Lee said, "I call down a Gypsy curse on everyone responsible for this crime." He walked away without looking back, adding simply, "We've come a long way since Runnymede."

Poised like mannequins, Gypsies sightsee in the Town Hall of Brussels after a reception in their honor.

66

NATIONAL GEOGRAPHIC PHOTOGRAPHER ALBERT MOLDVAY

$\mathcal{S}$*napping fingers, clapping hands, and whirling*
skirts attract a crowd before the Gothic Hôtel de Ville, or
Town Hall, of Brussels. Earlier, the Mayor formally welcomed
Gypsies for the first time in the city's history. An art gallery
honored the wanderers by exhibiting paintings of and by Gypsies.

*A Gypsy makes his violin cry. Schnuckenack Reinhardt,
in a Heidelberg recording studio (above), played for Pope Paul VI
on the Pontiff's birthday. His reward: a fiddle inscribed with
a variant of his name. At right, his son Forello
strums himself to sleep in his caravan bed.*

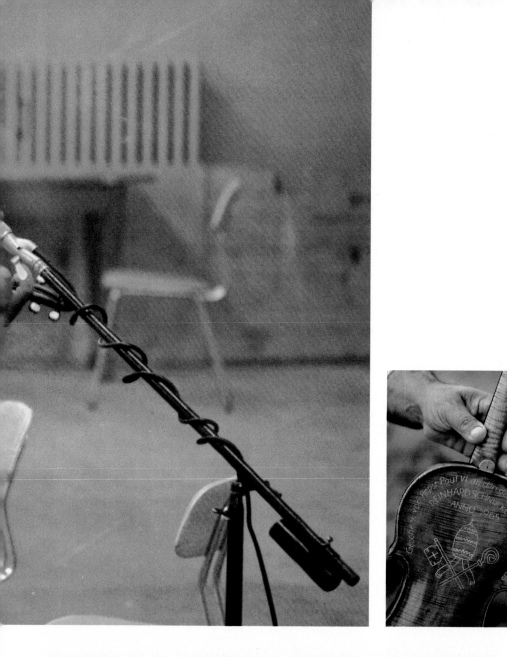
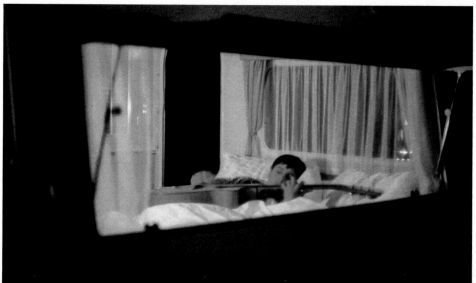

$\mathcal{F}$iles of poplars flank solemn Gypsy children beside
an irrigation canal at the edge of the Black Forest. Water
from a rustic trough (right) quenches a boy's thirst.

"I call down a Gypsy curse on everyone responsible for this crime," exclaimed Clifford Lee at Dachau. A stark sculpture there memorializes victims of Nazi concentration camps, among them untold thousands of Gypsies. One who escaped: a man whose forearm (right) bears a tattoo from the Auschwitz death camp.

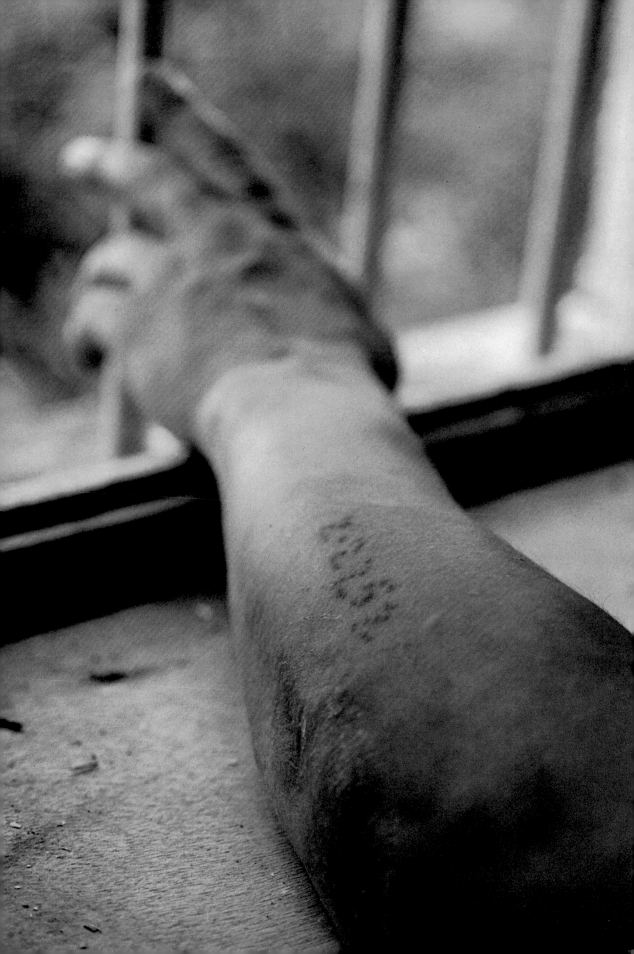

Beside the Danube in Czechoslovakia, Lee strums a guitar borrowed from a Gypsy child.

'In Summer... a Golden Life'

O N OUR FIRST NIGHT IN PRAGUE I slept in a gutter. We had arrived one Saturday midnight too tired to pitch camp; the Lees and Bruce found hotel rooms, and I slept in my camper bed, parked in the gutter on Wenceslas Square. I awoke as pious Czechs were making their way to early Mass — and stopping to peer curiously into the camper.

"A good Gypsy way to meet Czechoslovakia," chuckled Dr. Jiří Lípa when we looked him up a few hours later. Dr. Lípa, a linguist with the Czechoslovak Academy of Sciences, is the leading authority on the languages and customs of Czechoslovakia's estimated 300,000 Gypsies. Yet he seemed as interested in our camper as any of these early-morning visitors. "No, I've never camped out in my life," he said, "but I happily accept your invitation to travel with you. Should we start with Gypsies here?"

So we began with Prague, in an old apartment building a few feet from the famous Church of St. James. Here lived several families of Gypsies. One couple, the Feros, occupied a dark but exceedingly neat apartment. They fetched us beer —*pivos,* they called it.

"Hey," exclaimed Cliff. "In England we call a drink of any kind *piv*."

"A coincidence," said Dr. Lípa. "That's not one you Gypsies stole, but you picked up many Slavic words on your way through here!"

Cliff found other expressions from this part of the world in his own speech: his words for tavern and bed, for pipe, boot, and stockings, for body and vein—even for frost and thunder and lightning.

"The Feros speak pure Romany," Dr. Lípa explained. "We can classify our Gypsies by dialect into five kinds: Slovak, like these people; Hungarian; Rumanian, including the coppersmiths and the horse traders; a German group, or Bohemian Sinti—very few survived the concentration camps; and troughmakers who speak Rumanian, Hungarian, and Slovak —and claim not to be Gypsies at all. None are wanderers anymore; that way of life was banned in 1958. Now we must see some of each."

We were off, traveling throughout the city, meeting all sorts.

One man looked like a maharaja. "He acts like one, too," said Dr. Lípa. "Once, when he felt rich, he hired a boat on the Vltava River and a full orchestra to play for his friends. And his father! He was known as 'The Gentleman'; at fairs he wore 100-crown notes in his hatband."

We met some Kalderash—coppersmiths. In one little apartment a woman with splendid gold teeth called in a friend to play music for us on his guitar. We danced the czardas in her kitchen beneath a portrait of Joseph Stalin—and she toasted the United States in Russian vodka.

"Oh, you find everything among Gypsies," said Dr. Lípa, "and now we will visit some who are not angels."

So we called on the Queen of the Apartment Thieves. I shall not reveal her name, for she is a gentle, gray-haired soul and long retired from her profession.

"She will serve you a dish for dinner that is a Gypsy delicacy," said Dr. Lípa. While Her Majesty set the table, we talked. And thus we learned about a non-Gypsy woman who once fell in love with a Gypsy thief.

"She wanted to prove her usefulness," said our hostess, "and she became reckless in her thievery. The police found her trail and even pursued the couple with dogs."

"Were they caught?" asked Cliff.

"No, they escaped," said the Queen, "praise the Lord."

In the same spirit Cliff confessed some trespasses of British Gypsies.

"Did you people ever *drab* the *bawlo?*" he asked, meaning "poison the pig." Cliff explained the trick: Dip a flat-pressed sponge in melted lard; when it cools, feed it to a farmer's pig. Overnight the lard melts and the sponge expands, blocking the pig's digestive tract and killing the animal. "Then the Gypsies come to the farmer," said Cliff, "and beg the dead pig for their dogs. Of course, they eat the pig themselves. Old British Gypsies say it's the world's best meat."

"We always fed the pigs broken glass," said the Queen.

I picked at my meal, wondering what a biopsy might show. "Do not worry," said Dr. Lípa, smiling. "That dish is made from the ovaries and other organs of chickens."

As we took our leave of the Queen, Clifford, ever the courtier, whisked off his prized silk scarf and presented it to our hostess. She, in regal turn, gave each of us a present. Mine was an antique pewter crucifix—small enough to have come from an apartment.

Winding through Czechoslovakia from urban Prague to industrial Košice, the author meets coppersmiths and a Gypsy writer, and seeks Great Ida castle.

"And now," said Dr. Lípa as we drove to the outskirts of the city, "you must meet my best Gypsy friend: a genuine Bohemian Gypsy. They are almost extinct, so when I found him, I felt like a paleontologist stumbling upon a living mammoth."

He resembled a banker: a gray-haired, bespectacled, well-dressed gentleman named Václav Weinrich. Today, he owns a roof-repair business with his brothers. But he remembers his boyhood in a horse-drawn caravan. "And he writes his memories in his own Romany," Dr. Lípa added. "He writes unpolished truth, the way primitive artists paint — naively, vividly. In his own words: 'I tell everything so, as it was. I do not exaggerate. On the contrary, I reduce, because everybody has something he cannot tell. . . .' He calls his memories *How We Lived.*"

THUMBING THROUGH THE MANUSCRIPT, Dr. Lípa translated portions of it for me while the Weinrich family fed us supper one night. And here I quote parts of this curious, nostalgic document, for it reveals in singular fashion the old Bohemian Sinti Gypsy way of life, a style that vanished entirely three decades ago:

"I am born November 15, 1927. My father was a horse dealer and knife grinder, and he also had a merry-go-round and a shooting gallery that he took to fairs.

"We were 14 children. I went to school wherever our caravan was parked. But my best teacher was my mother's brother-in-law, a half-Gypsy. He had finished school. From him I learned to be fond of books, and I even wished to become a pediatrician or an attorney. But my father always had many horses and I had to care for them. Both in summer and in winter I had to go beg hay for the horses. And there are not so many hairs on my head as the number of times I have begged bread on the streets of a village.

"In summer, of course, we had a golden life. In the fields there was everything we needed. But in winter life was hellish. As soon as we came into a locality we had to go to the mayor with our registration books. Then we had to go to seek a stable for our horses, and get fodder and firewood. When we could not get a stable, our father pulled the feather quilts off us children and covered the horses with them. Many times it happened that in the morning the hair of our heads had frozen to the walls of the caravan. But we nevertheless loved that life....

"In the springtime our women filled the coops under the caravans with chickens. Their wings were clipped so we could identify them. Many times the police came to our vans while chickens were boiling in our pots. When the police asked after their origin, our women showed that we had chickens of our own in the coops—chickens of every color. This variety was necessary too, for sometimes the police came seeking chickens that got lost in the village. If they found, near our caravans, feathers that were the same color as the lost chickens, we could show them similar chickens in our coops....

"Each evening the men groomed the horses and talked with the peasants who came by. We made many swaps of horses when we stood with our vans on the village square. Always peasants came to us wanting to trade.

"If the nights were warm, we did not make a fire. The men sat down in the hay near the horses, smoked cigarettes, and talked with the peasants until the last of them went away. Then the conversation continued among ourselves.

"Finally, when the clock on the church tower struck eleven, my father would stretch. 'Tomorrow I have to go to the farrier's with a horse; today it cast a shoe. Good night, fellows!'

"Each night he went to check our cart and to look at the horses. And he went behind the caravan to make sure the hen coop was well shut and the dog securely tied. What if we had to leave in the night?

"Then, when he lay down on his bed, he put a hand behind his head and, with a lighted cigarette, he listened to horses eating oats and to frogs croaking in the village pond. After the day's troubles he liked this moment very much. This day had passed safely. And why think of tomorrow? Only the great God knows what tomorrow will be."

Generations removed from an open campfire, Yuray Pala and his wife live in comfort in an apartment in Prague. They and thousands like them once occupied huts outside villages.

Throughout Mr. Weinrich's memoirs Bohemian Sinti superstitions and folklore repeat like a musical theme. A kinsman Matrouzi, for example, warns young Václav against certain foods: "Every hen gets frightened when somebody catches her. And if you eat her heart, you will also get frightened when you fight."

We read about the *mulesko chiriklo,* "the bird of the dead," or owl—a bad omen among the Sintis. From his grandmother, Václav learned how a cousin heard the owl hoot one night and threw three embers at the bird to drive it away—and died within three days.

Of all Václav Weinrich's tales, two stand out with special meaning. One is his account of a violent battle with peasants in a village near Nitra, Slovakia, in the 1930's. It began one autumn when his Aunt Hanka saw some people slaughtering a hog just outside the village and tried to barter for part of the meat. When she entered the yard, a woman came out of the house, and, without saying a word, slapped her face.

"My aunt struck back," Weinrich wrote, "hitting the peasant on the head with a pot. But the peasant woman was in a family way, and she fainted. When her husband saw what had happened, he rushed at my aunt swinging the same butcher's ax that he was using to quarter the hog.

"Another woman ran out of the house and held the peasant back, and instantly my aunt ran out onto the road. Uncle Viniter, seeing the trouble, seized a stick and jumped down from the caravan. My mother's brother, Uncle Feri, jumped down after him. By now the peasant had struck the woman who had been holding him back, and, with the ax in his hand, ran to the gate. Uncle Feri struck him on the head with a caravan prop. The peasant tumbled down backward into the yard, quite unconscious, and the peasant woman began to shout that he was dead. This was the beginning of what followed.

"Now other peasants, alarmed by the cries, began to gather. When they saw that one of them had fought with Gypsies, they ran back to their yards, and everyone seized whatever he could find: pitchforks, axes, scythes, sabers. But neither did our men wait any longer. Each one reached behind the kitchen range in his van and seized a weapon. Old Yotsi jumped out of his caravan with a heavy army saber flashing in his hand. He wore no coat, just a shirt and vest, and a kerchief on his head, tied in back. To me, he resembled a typical ancient knight. He looked around and exclaimed, 'Men, keep your backs to each other! That way they'll not separate us!'

"OUR WOMEN, too, were ready to fight with their own weapons. I watched from my grandmother's van and saw old Yotsi swing his saber to strike away a pitchfork that a peasant held with both hands. Suddenly I saw another peasant running toward him from the side. The man had an ax. But Linka, Yotsi's wife, advanced with a fork in her hands and struck the peasant on his head with all her might. The man fell on his back and lay still.

"Older Sinti children handed the men more weapons. By now Uncle Viniter was wounded in the head. Another of our men was also hurt and so was Aunt Maryana, my mother's sister. All the wounded were put up in my grandmother's caravan and we carried them to the doctor.

"But while we were at the doctor's, all the peasants in the village rose to arms. They sounded the alarm and rang the church bells. Soon our vans were surrounded by peasants. Some of them even got in, seized small children by the hair and threw them out. Some even threw out babies wrapped in their blankets.

"The peasants chased my father through the village, beating him badly. When they passed the mayor's house, my father jumped into the yard. The mayor came out, and begged the people to calm down. But they attacked even the mayor. With difficulty, the mayor managed to jump back into his house and lock his door. My father, left in the yard, was now dragged out onto the road. Again the peasants beat him. But my father saw that beside the road stood an open blacksmith shop. He wriggled free and leaped into the shop. But the blacksmith had just taken a glowing horseshoe from the fire. Seeing my father, he now roared, 'Stop, or I'll burn your chops!' And he held the horseshoe so close to my father's face that his whiskers began to burn. Thus my father was forced to stand at attention like a soldier while the peasants beat him once more.

One of the last of the Bohemian Sintis, a Gypsy recalls her caravan years. Most of her people died in concentration camps.

"Four cars of police came from Nitra, but even they had to yield to the peasants. Finally soldiers arrived and rescued us. Otherwise we would have been massacred there. There was plenty of blood on the earth on the village square, just as it is when hogs are slaughtered."

Hearing this account, I wondered how the Slovakian peasants could have beaten Gypsy women and thrown babies out of their caravans. But the other story might explain a measure of the bitterness between Gypsies and peasants. Weinrich records a bizarre tale told him by old Yotsi, "a story I heard from my late grandfather when I was small," as Yotsi explained—events that must have happened shortly after 1800.

Yotsi describes a lurid robbery carried out by a band of Gypsies, two of them brothers "and both of them excellent burglars." After carefully surveying the house marked for robbery, "the women made . . . some slippers from old sacks—that the men could not be heard when walking. Five men went on the night expedition, and each put a pistol into his pocket and a large knife or dagger under his belt (they preferred daggers for prying doors open), and each one carried a sack."

But on this particular night the robbers discovered that the house contained a dead man lying in state with candles at his head. One of the thieves, feeling prankish, moved the corpse into a hog trough and put a sausage in its hands.

"God will punish us!" warned one old Gypsy. But the young thief went ahead—and met violent death that night in a fall. Thus, the kind of life that alienated the peasants.

"Imagine," said Cliff in a proper British way, "if that dead man had been one of your family. A sausage in his hand!"

As we drove toward Slovakia, I said to Dr. Lípa, "We must find two castles. We want to see that of King Sigismund and the Gypsy castle from the famous lament."

Dr. Lípa knew both stories well. Sigismund, King of Hungary, Bohemia, and other realms, had given a letter of safe-conduct to one of the first bands of Gypsies entering western Europe in the 15th century. They carried that passport all over Europe—so that many French still call Gypsies "Bohemians." We sought the place where Sigismund had received that band.

Our other castle seemed less certain. Romantics tell of a song called the "Gypsy Lament," a ballad about a castle named Great Ida that once was defended by Gypsies, but was lost in a terrible battle. Gypsies still mourn the loss of Great Ida, say some folklorists, and every time their musicians play the lament, they weep bitterly.

Gypsy hospitality in a Prague home lures the author into the kitchen to learn to dance the lively and fast-paced czardas.

Dr. Lípa laughed. "There is no such song as the 'Gypsy Lament,' but I know Gypsies who, for a large enough tip, will play and sing a sorrowful song and pretend it is the lament. They wail. They carry on. But it's all a joke. The castle, however, is another matter. Slovakia has a village named for the Great Ida. We'll investigate."

We went straight through to Bratislava, 200 miles southeast of Prague, with only one unscheduled stop. Bruce was driving the Volkswagen when a hare darted across the road and died beneath our wheels. Behind us, the Land-Rover stopped dead in the highway. We backed up to offer help, but Cliff waved us on. "We just want to get that hare you killed," he explained. *"Kanengro* makes a wonderful stew!"

So the hare accompanied us to Bratislava. There Cliff and I talked with engineer Imrich Farkaš, head of the Slovakian Office of Gypsy Affairs.

"We have a plan to solve the Gypsy problem by 1980," he told us. "Our aim is social assimilation." Most of the nation's Gypsies live under the control of the Slovakian government—a federated twin of the Czech government. "And we still have 56,000 Gypsies who have no regular job or fixed house, and who do not send their children to school.

"More than half of our Gypsies are under 18 years old—and the young can be changed." Engineer Farkaš extracted a bale of typed paper:

"Consider the Gypsy hut. We have 100,000 Gypsies living in 7,900 huts—thus an average of six to eight persons living in about 50 square feet. Last year we liquidated 665 of those huts and sent 450 Gypsies to state-owned apartments." My mind wandered, with a romantic sadness, to the families who had moved from liquidated huts to those solid apartments. "Bird cages," Cliff muttered. Soon we adjourned from offices and reports, and sought fresh air with a family of troughmakers camped on the outskirts of town.

THEIR UNLIQUIDATED HOUSING was substandard; their sanitation fell below the norm. But they had a free-enterprise business of their own. Out of great poplar logs they carved troughs the size of bathtubs, which peasants would use for the scalding of slaughtered livestock. Hospitably, the troughmakers invited us to share their forested camp on the banks of the Danube.

Bruce charmed the oldsters by taking their pictures as they worked. Sheila talked with the women, and Cliff made friends with the youngsters—but he developed doubts.

"Are you sure these are real Romanichals?" Cliff asked Dr. Lípa. "Their daughters stay so close to strange men."

"The troughmakers deny any Gypsy blood," said Dr. Lípa, "but Indian elements in their Rumanian tongue reveal their Romany origin."

The father's name was Michal Molnár and he came from the Nitra district—the same area, I recalled, where young Václav Weinrich had seen that battle with the peasants.

"We spend our winters there," said one old man who was paring poplar shavings from an almost completed trough. "In summer we come here by truck, if we can find a driver who will give us a ride."

Their campfire crackled with poplar chips, and over it boiled a rich-smelling pot of Slovak cabbage cooked with tomatoes, paprika, and smoked ham.

"You must join us," said Mr. Molnár.

Gratefully we accepted. Bruce darted back to our camper to share some delicacies from our own larder: a cake bought in Prague, sausage from Germany, and even some old cognac from France. But he failed to bring plates and spoons—an omission we soon regretted, for the Molnárs owned no plates. All of us had to take turns using the only two spoons in camp. We dipped right into the common pot, then passed the spoon on to anyone who seemed hungry. "They *look* healthy," said Cliff uncertainly, "but our people would never eat this way."

As we prepared to leave, Mrs. Molnár filled a tumbler with our antique cognac, and lifted the glass in our honor. I assumed this was a stirrup-cup for the whole crowd, like our single pot of stirrup-stew. Not so. Cognac that had aged for 15 years disappeared in a single gulp. Watching the deed, Bruce seemed to age a bit himself.

As we moved across Slovakia, Dr. Lípa introduced us to Gypsy families he knew. "See the facial differences between the two kinds of Gypsies living here—those of the Hungarian group on the one hand and of the Rumanian on the other?" said Dr. Lípa in the village of Hájske. "Gypsies of the Rumanian group have high cheekbones and Oriental eyes."

Along the way we camped in fields and once in an orchard of purpling plums near the River Váh. We feasted on sheep cheese—*brynza*—and hare stew. Above us loomed the battered Gothic walls of Čachtice Castle, "the seat of a wicked woman who ruled this region," Dr. Lípa told us. "To preserve her beauty, that woman killed many local virgins and bathed in their blood."

But we were seeking other castles. "I have brought with me a copy of one of King Sigismund's famous letters of safe-conduct," said Dr. Lípa. "In the original Latin." He translated easily:

"We, Sigismund . . . King of Hungary, Bohemia, Dalmatia, Croatia and of other places . . . Our faithful Ladislas, Chieftain of the Gypsies and others dependent on him have humbly besought us . . . our special benevolence. It has pleased us to grant their request . . . If the aforesaid Ladislas and his people present themselves in any place within our Empire . . . we enjoin you . . . on your allegiance to favor and protect them in every way . . . And if any trouble or disturbance should arise among them . . . then none of you whomsoever, but Count Ladislas alone, shall have the power of judging and acquitting. . . ."

The document closed with *Datum in Sepus . . . Anno Domini* MCCCC-XXIII. "Where," I asked, "is Sepus?"

"That's the Latin form for the province of Spiš," said Dr. Lípa. "It's in eastern Slovakia—northwest of the city of Košice. But finding the right castle may not be so easy."

My guidebook referred to "a number of medieval castles and of chateaux especially in the Poprad, Torysa, Laborec and Slaná river basins." The list included 19 major castles, plus six "historic town reservations."

I don't know how many of them we tried; I stopped logging the castles after five failures. We sometimes found castles unidentified on our maps. Local peasants were not always sure of the names. We got lost, and only Bruce's homing-pigeon instinct kept us from wandering over the border into Poland. But the scenery impressed us: big, muscular mountains with tormented rocks.

Bruce's spirits rose and fell like a light meter with the presence of sunshine or cloud. Both morale and light were low one cloudy evening as we tried to find another promising castle near the town of Spišské Podhradie. "Very, very large," a Slovak farmer assured us. Darkness settled. A slow drizzle began to fall. But finally, with the spotlight on our car, we found it: a walled bulk on top of an apparently roadless hill.

"Why not drive up anyway?" said Bruce. We were disgusted enough to try. So, engines roaring, we climbed wet grass on the steep slope, now skidding, now grabbing. On the first level terrace midway to the top, we

Bohemian Sinti writer Václav Weinrich and his wife stand in a Prague doorway. Part of his account of his boyhood appears in print for the first time in this chapter.

stopped and pitched camp. "Too wet for a campfire," said Bruce. Usually Cliff would argue that assumption. He maintains, as a point of Gypsy honor, that he can build a fire on any rainy night. This evening, however, he settled for a butane fire on the Land-Rover range.

"Clifford, you'll have a faster pot of tea this way," Sheila said, "and you won't mind a quick meal out of tins tonight."

The drizzle made a slow, rippling percussion on the canvas overhead. Below us a constellation of village lights winked in a moving bank of fog. We ate quietly.

"Let's explore this castle," said Bruce at last. "I've a feeling this is it."

We set out, with flashlights and raincoats, climbing the hill where it disappeared into low cloud, picking our way to an arched entrance in the wall. We entered an old courtyard, and in the beams of our flashlight the earth seemed to have changed color.

"This ground is blood red," whispered Cliff.

"And it colors the shoes," said Dr. Lípa. He was eerily right. But before we could solve the riddle, a dog barked and a flickering lamp moved in a castle window.

"A guard!" said Cliff. "Come on, Bruce, let's get out of here, or we'll be *lelled*." In moments of stress Cliff reverts to Romany. To be lelled means to be taken or arrested.

We felt vulnerable. Our campsite could well have been illegal, and our presence suspect. So with quiet voices and dimmer lights, we picked our way back down the hill.

FOG HID US through the night, and we awoke cocooned in gray. "I feel like Macbeth," said Cliff. Disembodied voices floated around us, scraps of conversation from peasants in the tomato fields below and from other people above us.

"The voices up there sound like German," said Dr. Lípa. "And Swedish. And even English."

We climbed again, and found some students.

"No, the scarlet on the earth is not blood," said a pretty little Swede. "Only paint. A TV crew was here to film a fantasy—knights and horses and maidens with flowing hair. And red earth." She was a student of archeology working for the summer with a few dozen other students on the restoration of the castle. Could we talk to her professor? He stood nearby: Dr. Adrian Vallášek, directing archeologist with the Office for Conservation of Historic Monuments. We described our quest.

"This is most probably the castle you want," said Dr. Vallášek. "King Sigismund usually used this one as his residence on royal tours. Documents like that safe-conduct were rarely signed in royal towns. Probably he signed it here. As you see, the castle is large—the most spacious castle in Slovakia. We call it simply the Spiš Castle."

We climbed among its battlements, watching as masons restored walls, and scholars dug up the cemetery beneath a Gothic chapel.

"At least," said Cliff, as he surveyed the timbered Slovakian mountains and the soft fields of hay, "we know Ladislas had good camping spots."

So did we. One of our pleasantest sites on the way to Košice was a schoolyard in the village of Kysak. Engineer Farkaš had told us about a new 21-day summer camp here for 50 Gypsy youngsters, a program

Blond Slovak counselor returns the volleyball in a spirited game at a three-week summer camp on the Hornád River near Košice. Sent to the country as a reward for regular school attendance, Gypsy children gather around Cliff Lee, who soon encouraged them to join him in song.

planned by the Red Cross and supported by the Slovakian Government.

"Our very first camp of this sort," said the director, Professor Klára Vosčíková. "So far only two cases of homesickness."

We ate with the youngsters, and Cliff led them in noisy song. We talked with their instructors, and we followed them from reveille and toothbrushing and volleyball through lights-out. We camped, in fact, near their windows, so we heard them whispering about us long after bedtime.

"Fine, dedicated people," said Cliff as we drove away waving. "But a camp for Gypsy children! Seems like carrying coals to Newcastle."

We still had one castle on our itinerary: the one musically mourned in the nonexistent "Gypsy Lament," Great Ida. We inquired in the town named Great—or Veľká—Ida.

"Certainly such a castle existed," said an old gentleman we met on the street. "It appears on our town coat of arms. A man still lives in the house built over the ruins. I can take you there." And did the town of Veľká Ida still have Gypsies in it? "Yes, exactly 993 Gypsies, I have heard."

We looked back to where Cliff and Sheila had parked. At least 993 Gypsies surrounded the Land-Rover. We honked, and the Lees followed us to the garden of agriculturist Tibor Idrányi.

"Yes, you are standing upon the ruins of the so-called Gypsy castle," said our host with great delight. He showed us what was left of old battlements and a shallow dent of a moat, then took us inside to his large parlor. Hunting trophies stared down at us with glassy eyes. "My hobby is taxidermy," he explained. Then, while sipping old Tokay wine and avoiding the stares of stuffed elk and foxes, we heard the story of the Great Ida.

In 1557 an Austrian army swept through these then-Hungarian regions, taking one castle after another. Ferenc Perenyi, lord of this keep, wanted to save his castle but the only troops he could find were about 1,000 Gypsies. The Austrians duly laid siege to the castle. The Gypsies defended it bravely, but finally ran out of ammunition. On August 17, 1557, after a 20-day siege, the Austrians took Great Ida and destroyed it. That much of the story can be documented.

"But Gypsies always make things exciting," said Mr. Idrányi with a laugh. Legends grew up, and one found its way into a long poem by the Hungarian poet János Arany in 1851; in about 60 pages of verse, Arany used this theme to satirize the Hungarian politicians of his day. The poem tells how the Gypsies of Great Ida ran out of powder just as the enemy lifted his siege.

As the Austrians began to withdraw, the Gypsy leader shouted, "You good-for-nothings! If we had any powder, we could finish you off!"

Hearing these words, the enemy promptly returned to attack the castle again. Thus fell the Great Ida. But the victors showed a certain magnanimity. Instead of taking the Gypsies prisoner, the conquerors ordered: "Run, Gypsy, as fast as you can!"

They ran, wrote Arany, "so fast that they still must be running."

We needed the same kind of marching orders. Our visas would expire at midnight and it was already late afternoon. We bolted a supper of leftover hare stew, then raced across the Danube plain, returning to Bratislava. By night Dr. Lípa caught his train back to Prague, and we reached the Danube and the Austrian-Czechoslovakian border with exactly ten minutes to spare.

"We ought to celebrate," I suggested. "Don't boast too soon," said Cliff as the border guards approached to check our exit visas. "Remember the Great Ida."

"*Protect them in every way ...*" *stated the safe-conduct granted Gypsies in 1423, most likely from Spiš Castle, in eastern Slovakia. At right, the author examines a Gypsy passbook required until after World War II.*

*Windows open to the soft, warm
sunlight outside her Prague apartment,
Mrs. Pala gives a kiss to a neighbor's
child. A 1958 law bans roaming by
Gypsies. Under government-sponsored
programs they move into permanent homes,
send their children to school, and
adapt their ways to a sedentary life.*

*I*tinerant troughmaker Michal Molnár (above) camps
on the Danube near a stand of poplars.
With his adz he hollows the soft wood into troughs
that butchers fill with boiling water to scald
slaughtered pigs before scraping off the bristles.

*S*ummer world of the troughmaker's dark-eyed children in-

cludes the fragrance of poplar-chip fires, fishing in

the Danube, and exploring nearby woods and meadows. Linguist Jiří Lípa

told the author, "The troughmakers deny any Gypsy blood, but

Indian elements in their Rumanian tongue reveal their Romany origin."

*F*arm wagon at the village of Hájske serves as a feeding bin for
horses and as a Gypsy baby's momentary crib. For two
generations this man's tribe has lived a settled life here in housing ranging
from sturdy brick homes to an abandoned railroad car.
Leaning against a porch railing, a Gypsy lad (below) seems lost in daydreams.

Constitution Day, August 20: Fireworks burst near Budapest's floodlit Parliament Building.

'They Shy at No Audacity'

WE PAUSED in Vienna only long enough for Bruce and me to get Hungarian visas, for Sheila to hear a few waltzes, and for Cliff to recuperate from a stomachache.

"Imagine!" he scoffed. "Getting sick from hare stew!"

Even before Cliff felt quite steady, we hurried on down the Danube, for we wanted to arrive in Budapest for the national celebration once named for Saint Stephen and now called Constitution Day. The hurry was worth it. Stunting MIG's roared above the city. Airborne troops jumped in bright parachutes. Decorated boats paraded down the Danube.

Budapest boasts nearly two million people—one-fifth of all Hungarians. Most of them, including clusters of brightly dressed Gypsies, were on hand for the fun.

"You can read Hungarian history in our faces," said Professor József Vekerdi, an eminent linguist and Gypsy scholar who had joined us.

We examined faces in the crowd, and, yes, it was there: Fine, prominent noses distinguished many of the Magyars, whose ancestors came from the steppes north of the Black Sea a thousand years ago. Maybe, too, we could see a touch of Attila, the short and stormy Hun who had ruled this land in the fifth century. Or the slanted eyes of Genghis Khan's Mongols, who galloped onto the Danubian plains in the 13th century.

"It was widely believed that our Gypsies came with the Turks in the mid-1400's," added the Professor. "But actually they came years earlier —some documents put them here by 1415.

"Now *there,* the dark woman with the pleated skirt. She is a Gypsy, a Walachian, our most numerous kind. Perhaps 80 percent of all our Gypsies are Walachian. We cannot be sure of numbers. Hungary may have as many as 300,000 Gypsies. Note that the woman's forehead and nose form a straight, Aryan line. Others of our Gypsies—the musicians, as much a linguistic as an occupational group—are not always so easy to identify. They're sometimes lighter-skinned and dress and act more like the Magyars. Liszt, you know, was inspired by their music. You must hear their orchestras in our restaurants."

There seemed no better way to observe a holiday season. With a young anthropologist named Eva Valis we went restaurant hopping, sampling fine Tokay wine and splendid food: cold fruit soup, chicken paprika, rich goulash. And to season it all, we had the music of Gypsy orchestras.

We felt regal as the bands entertained us with violin, viola, cello, double bass, clarinet, and cimbalom. I could even perceive why early Hungarian Communists for a while after World War II had outlawed Gypsy orchestras as symbols of aristocracy. And, indeed, the tradition of Gypsy music reaches deep into Hungary's monarchic past. The Hungarian language even boasts special words for being entertained by Gypsy musicians —*cigányozni* (literally "Gypsying") and *cigánnyal mulatni,* which expresses "reveling with Gypsies."

"Recruiting officers for the Austro-Hungarian army had Gypsy musicians to stir the spirits of men," said Professor Vekerdi. "They played tunes called *verbunkos.* Similar music led troops into battle, like the skirling of the bagpipes of Scotland."

Now our orchestra interrupted us with a Liszt rhapsody, and our thoughts turned to the composer.

"They shy at no audacity in music so long as it corresponds to their own bold instinct," wrote Franz Liszt, whose own flamboyant style showed the influence of 19th-century Gypsies here. "The chief characteristic of this music is the freedom, richness, variety and versatility of its rhythms, found nowhere else in a like degree. They change ceaselessly, intertwine, intersect, supersede.... Now babbling and fleet like a bevy of giggling maidens, and now spurred and champing like a troop of cavalry...."

But not all of our gypsying involved the classic rhapsody. In other restaurants Sheila melted when violins played "Fascination" for her, and Cliff tapped the table when the cimbalom plinked a medley from the operetta *The Gypsy Baron.*

"Every Gypsy musician is a splendid artist," said Professor Vekerdi proudly. "Much of Liszt's own Gypsy music came from cafes like this. But Liszt was mistaken in thinking of it as Gypsy in origin. Actually it was embellished Hungarian music. Real Gypsy folk music uses no instruments. Singers are accompanied by stamping feet, clicking tongues, the tapping of spoons, and the rapping of knuckles on tables."

We soon sampled this folk music as taped by ethnomusicologist Rudolf Víg of the Hungarian Academy of Sciences: sad, slow *mesalako dyila*—or

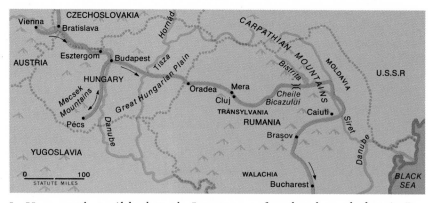

In Hungary the trail leads to the Lovara, once famed as horse dealers; in Rumania the author mingles with Gypsies in the mountains of Transylvania.

table-songs—and romping *khelimaske dyila* for dancing. We listened to the Stick Dance ("Peasants dance it, but only Gypsies sing the music") and the *pergetés*—songs using only syllables, like ta, ra, va.

"Now listen closely," said Dr. Víg. I first thought he was repeating the pergetés. "No, *that* one I recorded in India—a village in Rajasthan."

Perhaps no one has a better knowledge of Gypsy music than Rudolf Víg. Once the conductor of the Hungarian State Folk Music and Dance Ensemble, he speaks Romany and has personally recorded 3,000 of the 5,000 Gypsy folk songs in the academy collection as well as a thousand Indian and folk melodies.

"Jails play their part in this folk music," said Dr. Víg. "Gypsies exchange songs and compose new ones in prison, where they frequently find themselves for stealing."

Dr. Víg smiled. "Our great composer Kodály once asked me, 'Aren't you afraid of being robbed?' But I said no. On a train, a Gypsy might take my wallet. But as a Gypsy's guest—never! On one journey I lost a yellow pencil in a Gypsy village. Next day a child came bringing it to me—four kilometers away. They do not steal from friends."

Well, perhaps. Yet along the Danube there is no denying an outlaw tradition among many Gypsies. Romany words have enriched the argot of the gorgio underworld. And the willingness of some to do even the most despised jobs led to their being hired as executioners. Through history Gypsy hangmen have struck dread into the hearts of criminals.

Worse yet are the tales of Gypsy cannibals. Scholar Grellmann recorded newspaper accounts dated in September 1782 of "murderers and maneaters" in Hungary who had confessed that once at a wedding, they killed three people whom they ate. According to testimony, they preferred "the flesh of a young person from sixteen to eighteen years old." About 40 Gypsies were put to death in the case—some "broken upon the wheel...two of the most atrocious were quartered alive...."

Such tales of cannibalism have been frequently disputed. No less a personage than Joseph II, Emperor of the Holy Roman Empire, denounced the newspaper stories of 1782 and abolished trials of 150 other Gypsies imprisoned for the crime. Nonetheless, the newspaper reports of the confessions extracted under torture had resounded all over Europe, and the taint of cannibalism still clings to Gypsies today.

We stayed out of jails, but after meeting the honest and elite musician-Gypsies of Budapest, who are largely accepted in public, we visited some squalid Walachian Gypsies outside Esztergom who are not. Most of Hungary's Gypsies live in settled communities tidier than Esztergom. Wandering ceased when the state required them to settle after World War II, and the more inveterate rovers left the country.

"About 164 persons live in this neighborhood," said Eva Valis. "All poor and dirty." Miss Valis was entirely right. She had collected Gypsy folk tales there—stories of haunted castles, spells, and monsters.

"In the beginning I used a trick to win their confidence," Miss Valis said. "I would ask for a glass of water. They are surprised and pleased when an outsider will drink from their glass."

I followed the same tactic. The Esztergom Gypsies exuded a poisonous stench throughout the whole untidy neighborhood, but I managed to drink my fraternal glass of water without gagging. The gesture, or more likely the presence of Miss Valis, won us an invitation to dinner, which I had to decline—not too reluctantly.

Our trip to Pécs, 125 miles south of Budapest, was a different matter. We were seeking Lovári Gypsies, the tribe famous as horse traders.

"We in Hungary think Gypsies first became skilled horse dealers in the area that now includes our country and Transylvania," said Professor Vekerdi, who accompanied us. "Horse in Hungarian is *ló,* thus the word *lovári,* or horse dealer." Some authorities, however, believe Gypsies knew the trade much earlier, and that "lovári" may come from the Gypsy word for money—*lóve*—or perhaps from *lohari,* Hindi for blacksmith.

Today horse dealing by Gypsies is forbidden, but they do their best to elude officials and keep the trade going.

AT FIRST, in Pécs, we found few Gypsies. We wandered the old city, a university center for six centuries, and found only one Gypsy woman, working as a street sweeper.

Here in Pécs, late in the 15th century, King Ulászló II adopted 25 tents of Gypsy blacksmiths; they made weapons for the authorities. Later they even forged the tools used to torture a famous peasant rebel. The rebel's friends brought vengeance by impaling the smiths alive.

"Of course, we still have Gypsy smiths," the district personnel specialist, Mr. Weininger, told us in the town hall. "Others dig coal in the Mecsek Mountains. And we have many Gypsies on cooperative farms. But horse dealers? I know none."

Near the coal market, however, we met Imre Kovács, a Lovári Gypsy wagon driver and once an active horse trader. Minutes later we were enjoying his hospitality with several of his friends and relatives.

"The big horse markets are gone now, because of mechanization and the law," Kovács complained in his neat living room. "We mostly buy older horses and sell them for horsemeat. *Me* eat horsemeat? Never!"

An old saying here has it that "a Gypsy without a horse is no genuine Gypsy." These men were genuine, and soon everyone was telling historic tricks in selling the *grast*—horse in Hungarian Romany.

"If you have a quiet horse, flog him while shaking pebbles in a bucket; then you need only shake the bucket later and he grows mettlesome."

"Our folk," said Cliff, "sometimes hid a horse's gray hair with ink or with permanganate of potash. And to conceal an old horse's hollow eyes, they'd pierce the skin above the eye, insert a straw, and blow it up with air. Terrible tricks!"

The Lovara talked of masking the shortcomings of broken-winded horses — those with heaves.

"My father had such a horse," said Cliff. "He called it Old Moneybox. "A horse will start to heave and lose weight on dusty hay and musty oats, but he gets cleaned out and fattens on fresh pasture. Feedings of linseed cure the spasms. Father would fatten Old Moneybox, sell him to a farmer who he knew kept his horses shut in a damp stable where the symptoms would return. Then he'd wait a week or so and send another Gypsy to buy him back cheap."

"Do you know the oaths such dealers take?" asked Professor Vekerdi. "Our late scholar Kamill Erdős knew a dealer who would take a crucifix and swear, 'May my life dissolve if this horse is not a wonderful beast.'"

"Beware any Gypsy who takes such an oath," said Cliff. "They'll swear frightful things — 'May the Lord strike dead this child!' And it all is a barefaced lie. I know one old man — he takes off his hat, holds it beneath his face, and says, 'If that's not so, may me two eyes drop in this 'at!'"

Our talk of horses grew noisy. Wine and laughter spilled freely. We sang. And when we left, the whole Kovács family came out to wave and shout, *"Bahtalo drom!* Lucky road!"

LUCK LED US EAST, across the black alluvial steppes of the *csikós,* the Hungarian cowboy. We passed fat draft horses with braided tails and light-boned mounts with Arabian blood, then swarms of bicycles and carts. Fields were turning tan on the Great Hungarian Plain, for we were now haunted by a ghost of autumn. Soon we would look for ghosts of another sort, since the mountains of old Transylvania, once celebrated as the land of vampires and superstition, lay just ahead, in Rumania.

We crossed a border marked by a grassless minefield.

"I've a strange feeling about Rumanian Gypsies," said Cliff. "There was a family of them traveling in Ireland when I was a boy. Old Stankovitch Lazone was the father — he wore a great wiry mustache. Barbaric. The family slept in one caravan all together on the floor — men, women, children; my father thought it highly immoral. Stankovitch always carried a long knife. A fearless man, devoted to his family. When his wife died, Stankovitch was overcome with grief and bitterness. He took that long knife of his and went up into the mountains." Cliff paused. "Old Stankovitch was looking for God. And he took that knife *to kill God with.*"

We saw a Gypsy bird early in the afternoon. "It's really a pied wagtail," said Cliff. "It's true, you know, anytime you see a *romani chiriklo,* the Gypsy bird, you're sure to see Gypsies soon, even if you're in the heart of London."

We did, too. They were traveling down the road in a rickety horse-drawn caravan like a covered wagon, the first of many Rumanian Gypsies we met that afternoon. They shared the road with water buffalo pulling wicker wagons full of plums, for we had arrived at the harvest season.

Though wandering is not forbidden in Rumania, the government does try to make the footloose Gypsies settle down by forbidding them to trade in horses and by requiring that their children attend school. The result is that Rumania has some half-settled Gypsies. Judging from the number of caravans we saw during the afternoon, a good many appear to be somewhat less than half-settled. Those who are settled, however—and there are many—differ markedly from the rovers in language, customs, and beliefs.

We drove on after sunset, following the dark road from Oradea to Cluj. A scarlet moon rose over the Transylvanian hills, and by its ruddy light we found a campsite where a bridge spanned a noisy, rocky stream. The plum wagons creaked past us for hours as the moon bleached pale.

"It's a wet moon," said Cliff, "when a cloud cuts across it like that." We listened to the distant howl of a dog that evening, and our thoughts took an eerie turn. To us, conditioned by novels and old motion pictures, Transylvania is a place where folklore throbs with stories in the style of Count Dracula. By moonlight we watched for reveling witches and fairies, for a man falls ill and cursed if he steps upon their rings.

In the late 19th century Heinrich von Wlislocki wrote dramatically—and Dr. Lípa thinks fancifully—of the folklore of this land of seven lucky mountains, where you can catch snakes, frogs, or lizards and make them into potions with miraculous power. Graze your mare upon these slopes to make her fertile. Dig up the enchanted earth and eat some of it in hopes of achieving second sight in finding hidden treasures. Sprinkle it into a grave to ensure the corpse an easy passage to the "land of the dead."

Inside one mountain lives a legendary four-eyed bitch that you can often hear barking at a great distance. "One can sometimes see this bitch at a river quenching her thirst," wrote controversial folklorist von Wlislocki. "As often as she drinks, incessant rain sets on. Perhaps she corresponds to the bitch Sarama, of Indian mythology...."

But the charms of Transylvania also work as curses. "May the dogs eat thine heart on the lucky mountain," goes one malediction.

Soulful music played by a Gypsy primás, *first violin of an orchestra, evokes an uncertain response from a patron at a Budapest restaurant. The rich, rhythmic style of Gypsies deeply influenced Hungary's great Franz Liszt.*

"Once I tried a curse," said Cliff, "and the man died a few weeks later." It seemed a onetime friend of Cliff's had turned on him and called Gypsies "a parasitical lot." This happened a few days before Midsummer Night's Eve.

"At 12 of that Eve, you can take a piece of fruit," said Cliff, "and cut it with a silver knife."

"Do you say anything when you do it?" I asked.

"It's not what you say," said Cliff. "It's what you *think*. That man was dead in three weeks. Coincidence, of course."

Of course. Yet under that pale Transylvanian moon, Cliff did tell me the kind of fruit he sliced that other midnight. And I withhold that information, just in case some gorgio might be tempted to try the curse.

Next morning we found the effects of Cliff's wet moon, or perhaps of the lapping four-eyed bitch: We drove through dismal rain. But we also found, as Grellmann reported two centuries ago, that Transylvanian Gypsies "swarm upon the land like locusts." Today Gypsies throughout

Rumania number an estimated 100,000 to 200,000, including those who have been settled so long that they are considered "integrated."

Time and again we stopped at Gypsy camps, clusters of covered-wagon caravans with scraggly horses, black-bearded men, and women with long swirling skirts. I caught fleas on one such visit, and Cliff insisted that one girl-child tried to pick his pocket: "And she knew I was a Gypsy!"

They tried to buy Cliff's gold rings and his watch, and showed him their own gold. They even confided the source of their wealth. "They're illicit horse dealers, beggars, and thieves," said Cliff. But when he remarked that he was *bokalo*—hungry—a verminous old crone fetched him a generous mess of food.

AT LAST we reached Cluj, the mountain-rimmed capital of Transylvania and a city that straddles the two regional cultures. Most of the population speaks Latin-derived Rumanian; about a third speak Hungarian. Gypsies speak some of each, plus their own Romany.

One word especially had lured us here: *lavuta,* Gypsy for violin, adapted either from a Rumanian word or one that arrived with the Turks.

With two Cluj musicologists, Zoltán Kallós and István Almási, we went fiddle-chasing to a nearby village of Gypsy musicians at Mera. We arrived in town just as an old man on the street beat a small drum and shouted out a message. Though not a Gypsy himself, he was performing a task once traditionally shared with Gypsies.

"Our newspaper," said Mr. Almási. "The town crier has just announced, 'A buffalo has been killed, and the meat costs 16 *lei* per kilo.'"

In times past, Gypsies told fortunes here by tossing beans into circles drawn on the head of a drum. A logical idea, we could see, when a drum is associated with such important announcements.

The Gypsies of Mera lived on a steep hill called Balázsdomb, perched over the gorgio part of town. And here we quite literally fiddled away a day. We met Gypsy factory workers, hod carriers, mushroom gatherers, lace makers, and herbalists. Among the 150 families, we also talked with swarms of musicians and dancers—but not one beggar.

An old fiddler, Antal Feriárus, played, and his daughter danced the lively *chingerdyi,* clapping hands, smacking ankles, scuffing shoes on hard earth in rhythmic pattern. Since Hungary, we noticed, Gypsy music had taken an Eastern turn with sliding quarter tones, glissandos, and a kind of bagpipe skirl.

Cliff got carried away and began to dance with two women beside an aromatic pigpen. As the music rose and pulsed, I thought, "The Devil himself is here." Dr. Louis Krasno, the cardiologist and violinist, and a descendant of Transylvanian Gypsies, explains it this way: "When a performer and audience are united as one, then *Beng*—the Devil—visits the musicians and makes them play above their heads."

So did our hosts in Balázsdomb. And so did other Gypsies we encountered in villages and camps in eastern Rumania. We climbed to the wide, treeless Transylvanian Plateau, then crossed the Carpathian Mountains into Moldavia through a canyon pass called Cheile Bicazului. Along the roads we met Gypsy spoon-makers, spindle-makers, coppersmiths, wool dealers, merry-go-round proprietors, and knife grinders.

Many Gypsies declare that they are not Gypsies at all, but simply

Rumanians. Other Gypsies prefer colorful lies to such denials. "We are Abyssinians," insisted one obviously Gypsy family of swart spoon-makers. "And we build bridges in Turkey."

Sheila laughed: "But look at the way they walk—just like Clifford. A nimble, bandy-legged roll. See what a swinging stride they have, and how straight they hold themselves. You can always tell a Gypsy walk."

The Gypsy's long-standing low status here explains why he lies about his origins. After all, Gypsies were bought and sold as slaves in Moldavia and Walachia for 500 years—until the mid-19th century, when slavery was abolished in Rumania.

As late as 1852 a chronicler described the villages of Gypsy slaves in this way: "Their clothing consisted of a shirt of coarse material which they wore until it rotted.... The children went about completely naked. ...They slept everywhere.... a stinking collection of gaunt, half-naked, shivering creatures who came from the stables, kitchens, open sheds, from all directions...."

As the slaves were freed between 1834 and 1856, the old slave communities grew into the villages of settled Gypsies that now dot Rumania.

Whatever its harsh history, we much enjoyed the hospitable countryside. We bathed in icy streams, and camped where we liked—in cornfields, beside ski-lifts, in pastures where brown milk cows licked their calves.

"It's a loud silence here," said Cliff. "You know it's quiet when you hear the blood pulsing in your ears."

At Braşov, in the Transylvanian Alps, we were warned about the company we kept. A blue-eyed Saxon boy named Andreas told Cliff, "Gypsies are dirty thieves, and they sell brass rings for gold." Cliff laughed, identified himself as a Gypsy, and we went on. But on our way to Bucharest, we recalled the warning. Stuck on a bridge behind a slow Gypsy caravan, Bruce and I waved and got into a pantomime conversation with the family. They were selling a ring—and held up currency to show us the price. The charade looked like fun, so we pulled off the road to talk. Cliff at once began to bargain. "But just as a joke," he said. "I have no Rumanian currency."

When some gorgios came up, the young Gypsy holding the ring hid it and grew conspiratorial. Could he be a fence for thieves—or a black marketeer? Or were these people just selling brass? The questions seemed worth a small investment.

Suddenly, an old woman from the caravan approached me with a basket of fresh onions. Nesting beneath her produce, hidden from the eyes of any police, was another ring. *"Sunakai?"* I asked. "Gold?" She nodded vigorously. Whispering, we bargained. I slipped a 100-lei note (about $5) into the basket and picked up the ring. I didn't examine it closely until we stopped at the next gasoline station.

"You got one *too?*" whooped Bruce. He showed me his—an inscribed wedding ring. And Cliff had acquired a huge monogrammed ring that weighed down his hand.

"But how?" I asked. "You had no money."

"I traded," Cliff laughed, with triumphant relish. "This cost me my

"A Gypsy without a horse is no genuine Gypsy," goes an old saying. This Hungarian Lovári follows a long tradition of cunning with these animals.

watch. Don't worry—the rings are gold." Our success alarmed me: We either owned hot or black-market rings. I slipped my own ring onto a finger and wondered about research facilities in Rumanian jails. Yet, before we reached Bucharest, my mind was at ease: My finger was green.

"It's an alloy," Cliff insisted. "There's gold in these rings—not the quality of my sovereign, mind you. But gold. You can't fool a Gypsy about gold."

But by now, Bruce too had a green finger. Though the two of us put our rings away, Cliff continued to wear his around Bucharest.

In the crowded capital we visited with the city's famous Gypsy flower vendors. When we spoke Romany to them they gave us armfuls of flowers as gifts. By night we listened to the singing of some foggy-voiced Gypsy minstrels in restaurants. Their harmonies sounded so oddly Asian that I asked the Rumanian ethnomusicologist Gheorghe Ciobanu whether theirs might have been the famous Gypsy scale.

"It's in no way Gypsy in origin. Actually, it comes from the Persian-Arabic world by means of the Turks," said Professor Ciobanu.

"In the latter half of the 16th century, the Ottoman Turks began to appoint ruling princes in Rumania. Each new ruler received as a gift from the Sultan a Turkish band—a *mehterhanea*. So for two and a half centuries, Turkish music was heard at the courts of the two Rumanian principalities. The boyars—landed nobles—followed the princes' example, and those owning Gypsy slaves formed their own bands of *lăutari,* or minstrels, who sang and played Turkish music.

"It's interesting to note here that although the first mention of Gypsies in Rumania dates from the latter part of the 14th century, they don't appear in documents as folk musicians earlier than the 16th century."

Professor Ciobanu showed me a chronicle describing the "continuous banqueting with songs and all kinds of music every day" enjoyed by a Prince of Moldavia. The music passed to the lower classes, retaining its oriental character—the so-called "Gypsy scale"—and minstrels became very popular. One Prince had them "walk before him of a night-time singing love-songs."

Minstrels are disappearing today, Professor Ciobanu said. Those remaining—"and 95 percent of them are Gypsies"—often live in communities near the old boyar estates, traveling the countryside and playing at peasant weddings and feasts.

When I left the professor, I found Cliff parked on the street, actively bargaining with a Bucharest Gypsy. The subject was gold rings. "Not again!" I said.

"No," said Cliff, "he wants to *buy.* I'm going to keep my ring, but if you want to sell yours...."

The eager Gypsy customer grabbed my ring the moment I showed it to him. Nor would he return it. Finally, he pushed 150 lei at me and walked hurriedly away. "Too little," said Cliff, "but anyhow, you made a profit."

He spoke too soon. A moment later my customer was back, to say that the ring was "nix good."

"You gave back his money?" asked Cliff a little later. "A trade's a trade! If a man whines like that, we tell him to go and deal with the children."

But I was content. I wasn't carrying away stolen or black-market gold. Just a brass souvenir—and some satisfaction: How many other gorgios, even temporarily, have ever gypped a Gypsy?

A whole country his home, a Rumanian Gypsy rests with his son near the Carpathian Mountains before moving on.

Experts in the open, Rumanian Gypsies make camp while wandering in Transylvania. At upper left, a woman shelters beneath a sheet of plastic. Another camper savors the smell of cooking.

Glittering trove of gold coins and medallions — produced as if by magic from among old rags — intrigues Cliff Lee during a brief exchange with a Rumanian Gypsy. Children (above) tug at a motorist passing out candy. He had stopped to stare at a Gypsy camp — and ended up desperately trying to get away.

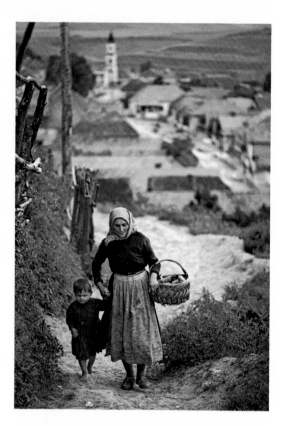

Lilt of a Gypsy fiddle sounds over the Transylvanian village of Mera. Cliff Lee joined the dancers in their spontaneous show of greeting. Her basket filled with freshly picked mushrooms, a Gypsy herb peddler and her daughter (upper left) climb a steep hill to Balázsdomb, Mera's isolated Gypsy quarter. The drum-beating town crier, a non-Gypsy, shouts out a message: "A buffalo has been killed, and the meat costs 16 lei per kilo."

Streaked with the grime of a squalid existence, a blond Walachian
Gypsy boy in the Danube Valley rests on the back of a discarded armchair.
A Hungarian Gypsy (opposite) stands outside his shantytown home
on the edge of the town of Esztergom. Wandering has ceased
since a state law required Gypsies to settle after World War II.

*W*ith *a hint of mischief in their eyes, Rumanian Gypsies signal*

the price of a promised bargain. Following by car, photographer Dale

stopped farther down the road with the author and Cliff Lee, where each

bought a ring. A Gypsy lad (above) rides the back of an

open wagon, and a Bucharest flower vendor offers prime gladiolus blooms.

*In a pensive mood, a barefoot Kalderash girl passes
the time on a carrousel while her father sells kettles
at a country fair. Small coins enhance her dark braids.
On the way back to his mountain village, a Gypsy
wool dealer (below) stops to rest after selling his fleece.*

Bulgarian Gypsy smiles a welcome to her village.

'Long Life to Everyone'

OUR STARS WERE CROSSED over Bulgaria. Among the Rumanian Gypsies, Bruce had caught a virus and I had caught fleas. We moved across the wide Danube, munching aspirin, scratching, and in no mood to celebrate Bulgaria's 25th anniversary of Communist rule.

We had been promised guides by Bulgarian officials, but they apparently had been reassigned. After an overnight wait in the city of Ruse, however, we found an English-speaking telephone operator, Mary Todoroff, through the tourist office. Mary had lived in Australia 12 years and had an Aussie accent. She would accompany us as interpreter to the hinterlands.

Most of the Gypsies we met were settled in pleasant, tile-roof country houses. Since 1958, Bulgaria has made regular employment compulsory, required education to age 15, and forbidden the wandering life. Yet on this warm September day we found a few forlorn families still on the move in open wagons, picking rose hips and herbs growing wild on the brushy slopes of the Sliven ("plum") Mountains. Dutifully, through the shimmering haze of his own fever, Bruce photographed the scenes. But Mary, an exemplary Communist Party member, seemed concerned that we might be gathering material for propaganda.

"I have never really known any Gypsies well," said Mary. And of Cliff and Sheila she asserted that they had done nothing to make her believe they *were* Gypsies. "You are different," she told Cliff. "You're a decent man." Cliff tried, with little success, to feel complimented.

Bulgaria has an estimated quarter million Gypsies, about 3 percent of its population of 8,500,000. Although the government officially opposes religion, half of the Gypsies are said to be Eastern Orthodox, and half Moslem. In 1877, when Bulgars rose against their Moslem Turkish rulers, Gypsies of both faiths joined the Christian patriots for the Battle of Shipka, a milestone on the road to Bulgarian independence.

Perhaps such credentials, along with the availability of higher education since 1944, have helped some Gypsies of Sliven — 50 miles east of Shipka Mountain — rise to the ranks of engineers, teachers, and physicians. When we met them, local Gypsies themselves gave public credit to Communist rule. So did the non-Gypsy officials who chaperoned us.

"Print no lies," demanded one splendidly strong Bulgar lady named Tsanka Georgieva Mihailova. "We do not forbid the Gypsies to speak their language! They are even permitted to speak it on the street." Cliff spoke with many, easily identifiable by their dark skin and colorful dress. "I can understand this Romany better than that in Rumania," he said.

As we drove through the countryside, we found individual Bulgars friendly and hospitable. Peasants gave us collective-farm plums and people's peaches. Only in the capital city, Sofia, crowded with visitors for the Communist holiday, did hospitality waver. Our promised rooms were replaced with substitutes; nothing was easy, and even photographing a Gypsy street sweeper stirred suspicion.

For two days we tried to find a Gypsy wedding. In the onetime royal palace — in a wing now housing the Museum of Ethnology — I met Dr. Ivanitchka Georgieva, an attractive young ethnologist who had written a paper on Gypsy weddings in Sliven.

"They resemble the 19th-century weddings of Bulgarian peasants," she said. "Some ceremonies are Turkish in origin, like the ritual Turkish baths for wedding guests and, on different days, for the bride and groom. Other traditions are Slavic: singing songs while sifting flour for the wedding bread, for example."

"Perhaps we can find a wedding for you to photograph," suggested one Gypsy. So we followed him from a downtown restaurant hangout for actors to distant apartments. We found Gypsy musicians playing goatskin bagpipes (the Bulgarian *gaida)* and accordions. But no weddings.

We had better luck finding the Gypsy newspaper, a tabloid called in Romany *Nevo Drom,* or "New Road." I reached the city room in a fourth-floor walk-up. Some newsmen were seated around a large table singing.

"Partisan hymns," Mary explained. "They celebrate the Liberation."

We found the editor of *Nevo Drom,* Eshua Kemalov, and called him away from the songfest. "Yes, we started with 2,000 subscribers 11 years ago and today have 15,000. We once had a circulation of 40,000, but now paper is rationed. With a price of 24 *stotinki* a year [about 12 cents U. S.] we have no problem getting subscribers.

"We publish once a month and have a staff of three: A Bulgarian — myself — a Jew, and a Gypsy girl in her 20's who is a journalism graduate."

We skimmed headlines of the latest issue, written mostly in Bulgarian: "Long Live the Socialist Fatherland"..."A Quarter-Century Road"... "Measurements of the Revolution."

By now a parade was forming in the streets, and we were eager to leave Sofia before traffic and barricades walled us in. So we waved goodbye to Mary and headed northwest toward the Yugoslav border, 35 miles away.

Bruce looked thoughtful. He had slipped away the day before with some Rumanian tourists on an afternoon's drive south to see the monastery at Rila, founded in the 10th century. "Near there I met a family of Gypsy brickmakers," he said. "And the father was building a cart. I asked if he planned to go back on the road. 'No,' he told me, 'it is forbidden.' Then he looked very sad — homesick, really — and said, 'This cart is just for the children to sleep in.'"

W̶E ARRIVED in Skopje, Yugoslavia, in need of a hotel laundry. On our route south from Niš, as we visited a few groups of settled Gypsies, we had been camping out, living off the land and the hospitality of peasants who gave us eggs, cheese, homemade brandy, and fruit. *"Dosta,"* Cliff had said. "It's our word for 'plenty,' and they use it here. Maybe in this friendly country we poor Gypsies first learned what 'plenty' meant."

At least we were plenty dirty. So we checked into a new hotel for rehabilitation. Almost everything in the center of this capital of the Socialist Republic of Macedonia is new, and herein lies a tragic tale.

At the dim hour of 5:17 a.m. on July 26, 1963, sleeping citizens were wrenched awake by the sickening rumble of an earthquake. During the next terrible hours, severe quakes continued to rock the city, the sharpest registering 8 on the 12-point Mercalli intensity scale. Hundreds of tremors were recorded before the earth finally quieted down months later.

More than 1,000 people were killed, 10,000 were buried alive and later rescued, and 200,000 were left homeless. Yet Skopje, 75 percent destroyed, rose again. In addition to massive building efforts by Yugoslavs themselves, help came from 78 other countries. The British sent prefabricated housing; Americans brought a complete hospital and metal Quonset huts; Russians gave a factory for prefabricating homes. To an outlying Quonset-hut community called Shuto Orizare came a number of long-settled Gypsy families from the wreckage of their old town quarter.

"After the first Roms went there, some Macedonians, Turks, and Albanians sold their houses to more Roms and moved out, and Shuto Orizare became mostly a Rom settlement," said 32-year-old Abdi Faik, a Gypsy and a deputy in the Macedonian Parliament.

Today Shuto Orizare is home to some 23,000 Gypsies — "the world's largest Gypsy town," Skopje Romanies proudly claim. "It's the only place where Gypsies aren't a minority," laughed the young deputy.

In two days we felt like old settlers. At a feast arranged by Abdi Faik we visited with engineers, professors, artists, chemists, Communist Party functionaries — Gypsies all. And over strong drink and pork our informally

Settled Gypsies succeed in gorgio jobs. In Skopje, Yugoslavia, Professor Saip Jusufovski leads calisthenics at an industrial training school. Engineer Tefik Asan and secretary Fikria Dimirovitch do work long shunned by the Rom as too confining. Dr. Sabi Yordanoff, a Bulgarian Gypsy physician, examines X-rays at a hospital at Sliven. In Skopje's Shuto Orizare, possibly the world's largest Gypsy community, live engineers, technicians, and Communist Party functionaries.

Moslem hosts told us about their ways. A poet-teacher named Saip Jusufovski read a composition in Romany, a sad poem about roving Gypsies titled "They Don't Stay in One Place." Next, a successful young Gypsy singer and recording star, Muharem Serbesjovski, sang *"Djelem, Djelem,"* a Gypsy song meaning "I Went, I Went."

Over the applause, I asked Deputy Faik the same question I'd been repeating since Germany: "Do you know of any Gypsy weddings soon?"

"Yes," he said. "Six this weekend. Come here tomorrow at 4 p.m."

Next day, when I arrived, I saw a crowd forming outside one house and hurried to investigate—just as pallbearers carried out a coffin. Across the street a brass band was tootling happy dance music. Was this someone's idea of a joke?

"No, two different things," a bystander explained. "The band is for a wedding across the street. The old man died yesterday. He was Djemail Hedip, perhaps 80 years old."

I started to photograph the all-male procession, but a grieving son waved me off. The *hoja,* or Moslem priest, conspiratorially beckoned me to follow along with him. "I am Durmish Serbesjovski," he whispered, "father of the singer you met yesterday. Just wait." We climbed the hill behind town, our pallbearers moving slowly under the green coffin.

At this point Bruce drove up, and I filled him in. "O.K.," he said, "I'll get the whole procession with a long lens." Bruce drove off in search of his vantage, as we climbed the hill.

Among old gravestones we halted, and the pallbearers lowered the coffin to a cemetery bench. The men then sat down and lighted cigarettes. It was an utterly Gypsy gesture and it made me think of the Welsh mountainside funeral of the great English Gypsiologist John Sampson, when Cliff's grandfather Ithal Lee lighted his pipe from the burning wooden box which had held Sampson's ashes.

Soon our rested pallbearers stood, and the priest keened a prayer across the valley. We proceeded upward to the spot where a crowd of male relatives had assembled around a new grave. The bearers opened the coffin—which would be used over and over—removed the sack-clad corpse, lowered it into the grave, and shoveled in dry earth.

"May I take pictures now?" I asked. The bereaved son's manner brightened. He even posed. So I made a record of the graveside proceedings.

Now the priest, singing an incantation, poured water from an earthen flask upon the dry dirt. This was the solemn *talgin al-mayit,* when the dead man is given instructions for answering the angels of the tomb. At this holy moment, Bruce's guide-translator appeared at my side. "The authorities have seized Mr. Dale," he said. "And they want you."

"What *for?*" I whispered.

"This cemetery is located on a military reservation," said the guide. "You have both taken pictures."

I proceeded down the hill to give myself up, and found Bruce being guarded by soldiers with submachine guns. "The civilian police want us too," he said. "They're arguing to see who gets us."

Soon Cliff and Sheila drove up to ask what was keeping us, and to report that wedding dances had started. While the officers all talked, Sheila put her kettle on the burner. A moment later she was pouring everyone proper British tea straight from her Land-Rover kitchen. Perhaps she used some Gypsy philter, for in five minutes the officials announced, "You may go. But no more military pictures."

We solemnly promised and dashed downhill to join a wedding feast.

From Bucharest the pursuit of Romany heritage leads to university-trained Gypsies in Bulgaria, weddings in Skopje, and a Gypsy village in Greece.

A ten-piece orchestra was playing brassy music; the street had filled with an Arabian Nights multitude. Women wore the Turkish *şalvar,* baggy harem pants of diaphanous material. Their foreheads were adorned with *peche,* as Gypsies here call the tinsel-jewel ornaments.

A dancing lady handed me a beer as she passed. I swigged, then she whisked the bottle back to share with another reveler.

In the rosy light of sunset, dancers snaked through the street; whenever the musicians stopped for breath, the sounds from other wedding orchestras wafted in like echoes.

"Welcome! I am the father of the groom," said a strapping thick-necked fellow named Mustafa Asip. "Meet my son, Haidin." The groom, dressed up in a new suit, was all of 14 years old, the same age as his bride.

"I work as a tailor, like my father," Haidin explained. "My fiancée —Gulja Seferova—can't come to our wedding feast." He laughed at my social ignorance, so I asked a pretty secretary, Fikria Dimirovitch, for a crash course in weddingology.

"Yes, it all starts when parents arrange the marriage. Rings are exchanged maybe a year before the wedding.

"Then, a few days before the ceremony, the boy's family dyes the girl's hair with henna. And the bride cries. Next day, women of both families take the bride to the bath; they sing, eat pies and cheese, and tell jokes.

"Now with *this* wedding—about nine o'clock tonight, all the people here will make a procession to the girl's house. And the boy's family will put henna on the girl's hands to dye them— a mark of piety. Tomorrow, on Sunday, you see the real procession: The groom's family goes to the bride's house and takes her to the new one he is building. But all this you'll see. Now you must eat."

Striding toward the camera, a man in Sofia, bent on protecting Bulgaria's image, demands that Bruce Dale stop taking photographs of a Gypsy street sweeper.

Along the street a table stretched at least 100 feet; only men ate here. The women, some with suckling infants, ate at another long table near the groom's house. At least 400 people were feasting on lamb stew, bread, and beer, courtesy of the groom's father. We joined them. Suddenly the bride's grandfather came up in great excitement.

"Can you drive a child to the hospital in Skopje?" he asked. "Ill, very much fever...." We hurried away from our banquet table to a spot where a four-year-old boy was doing a faltering dance with his old grandmother.

"Now," she said, "you have had your dance, so you can go." Fun should come before hospitals, everyone agreed. So young Mustafa, his head sizzling with fever, climbed into our camper for a flying trip to town. Luckily, it was only tonsillitis, so we were able to rush back in time for the evening procession.

The orchestra led us. One man cavorted with a wine bottle. Girls tapped spoons in rhythm. And others shouted in Turkish, *"Yashasin! Long life to everyone!"*

Outside the bride's house—a Quonset hut cheerily adorned with crepe-paper flowers—I waited among great caldrons of steaming food. But Bruce slipped inside the door, the only man there, to record the ceremony on film.

Soon the henna crowd emerged from the bride's house, and our friends suggested a different party entirely. So we next attended a noisy bash with 1,500 guests. "Where is the happy couple?" I asked.

"The wedding here is over," said our Gypsy guide. "So the musicians and food serve a second purpose: As Moslems, the bride's younger brothers must be circumcised. This is a circumcision dance."

The two boys—Hashim, age seven, and Tefik, six months—waited sleepily nearby. Next morning, after the ritual operation performed by a barber, the boys would return to a room sumptuously decorated for their convalescence.

Meantime, to the sound of Yugoslavian *zurla*—a long, straight horn—and tambourine, the dancers roared on. Women sprinkled the dusty street with water. Plum brandy, Turkish raki, and beer flowed with non-Moslem abundance. But we couldn't go another round. In about five hours we had covered a funeral, a hospital visit, a wedding feast, and a circumcision dance—"with time out to get arrested," Bruce added. So we slipped away, like dull gorgios, to go to bed.

The bride was to change houses on Sunday afternoon, and we returned then to the Asip house to watch the procession that would go to fetch her.

"Gypsy wedding customs follow the fashion of the land we're in,"

Moslem funeral of a Skopje Gypsy reaches its most solemn moment as the priest pours water on the grave and exhorts the deceased: "Let them [the angels] not ...terrify thee...And when they ask thee, 'Who is thy Lord and who is thy Prophet...?' then say, 'God is my Lord and Muhammad my Prophet....'"

said Cliff as we waited. "My grandparents had a broomstick marriage in Wales." In that ceremony Gypsies jumped over a branch of flowering broom. "But Sheila and I were wed in a little Catholic church in Ireland. We barely had a ha'penny, for I'd lost my money gambling."

"Both families disapproved," Sheila added. "But my mother and sister slipped in the back of the church to watch."

"I gave two Irish half crowns to the acolyte," Cliff continued, "but the priest took pity on this poor Gypsy and made him return them. I still have the coins—inscribed with our names. And that night we went to a boardinghouse—the first night I'd ever spent in a house."

Band music blared, and the procession formed. Leading us was the bearer of a long pole festooned with wedding presents of shirts, pillowcases, and bolts of cloth. We marched noisily to the bride's street, where a crowd of relatives had erected a barricade. Laughing, the bride's people shook sticks, axes, and shovels in our faces. Not until the senior Asip had bargained for the bride and paid a toll of brandy and beer did his in-laws bring down the barricade.

Veiled and in tears, the bride emerged from her house. Women relatives lifted the veil to kiss her. Others tucked banknotes as presents into the hatband of the maid of honor. With music so loud it was almost visible, we returned to the newlyweds' house, where the groom waited at the gate. As we arrived, he tossed candy to the crowd, while a groomsman, following tradition, carried a mirror before the bride.

Now the bride stood inside the ribbon-decked doorway, and her new relatives gave her a loaf of bread, symbol of their support, and smashed a small cup—to break with the past. The mother-in-law fed the girl sweets. Everyone went indoors, and the musicians lighted cigarettes.

"Why didn't the bride speak?" I asked.

"It's forbidden," said the guide. "She can't speak until tomorrow."

"What a fine wedding present for the groom!" said Cliff.

The party would continue until a groomsman could carry news to the bride's family that the girl had proved honest and was accepted. Then there would be more brandy and gifts for the attendants.

BUT OUR WAY LED SOUTH, along the muddy Vardar River, through tunnels, past cotton fields, tomato harvests, and packtrains of donkeys. Then the valley widened. We cleared customs again and entered a sunny land of whitewashed houses and red tile roofs: Greece.

Cliff the classicist felt quite at home. In Salonica he got his first look at distant Mount Olympus—then climbed straight to the local acropolis and found a colony of Gypsies.

"Half of us come from Asia Minor, and the rest from Greece," said Athanasios Christoforou. "No rovers. And all of us are Christian."

We saw other Gypsy neighborhoods, including one called Texas ("because they drink more and fight more," according to Mayor Alexander Constantinídes), and an area outside town famous for Gypsies with dancing monkeys.

Our goal was Flámbouron, a village 40 miles northeast, near Nigríta.

"Once we were fishermen and basketmakers here," said the village patriarch, Nikolas Kulialis. "But in 1932 our lake dried up. Well, in 1934 the Greek government gave us the drained land to farm. A better life. We raise tobacco, corn, beans—yes, about 1,700 of us are Gypsies, and 300 are Greeks who used to be wanderers."

Neat homes showed that Flámbouron had lace-curtain Gypsies. "And the very first Gypsy policeman I've ever seen!" said Cliff.

Yet, for all the village's progress, Flámbouron Gypsies still cling to some old ways. Here we met an aged sorceress called the *ababina*. Mr. Kulialis said she was 88 years old. "No, 90!" she corrected. She pronounced her words through only two teeth and in a voice shattered by time. But her eyes shone clear. "Sorcery? No, no," she objected.

Then Mr. Kulialis explained, "She has been in trouble with the church." He described how the ababina and some apprentices—all widows or spinsters—dance wildly around the sick, chanting to cure them.

When we departed, Cliff bade the ababina a respectful farewell: *"Ja Develesa, puri dai.* Go with God, old mother." She smiled, exposing her two enduring teeth like a benediction.

In the mid-19th century, Greece produced one of the great Gypsiologists, A. G. Paspati, a physician and a student of Sanskrit. "After repairing to different Gypsy haunts in Constantinople and its suburbs, and mingling with the people," and using "money as a spur to their sluggish memory," he published an important Romany dictionary. His work on the origin of the words used by European Gypsies helped later scholars—and now us—trace the Gypsy trail.

The road from Nigríta took us back to the sea, and we looked across the Aegean to tall Mount Athos. A Georgian monk there in the year 1100 wrote of some "Atsíncan," describing them as descendants of Samaritans. Some scholars doubt these Atsíncan were Gypsies, but John Sampson noted they were "wizards and famous rogues, and, incidentally, adepts in animal poisoning." Obviously, bad Samaritans, and the name *Tsincan* stuck to the Gypsies.

For certain we know that Gypsies reached the Greek islands by 1322. An Irish pilgrim wrote of seeing them on Crete that year at Iráklion. And from the large number of words the Gypsies borrowed, it seems clear that their stay among Greek-speaking people was very long. Their word for time and season, *cheros,* came from the Greek *kairós.* They picked up metalworking and smithy words for copper, kettle, nail, horseshoe, and tongs. And they adopted the Greek *drom* for "road." "Perhaps these were their first *good* roads," suggested Cliff. "A Roman legacy."

Under the clear sky of Greece, Gypsies found a word for heaven—*ravnos.* But *trushul,* the Romany word used by some for "cross," seems different in origin. Paspati suggested that this word might be related to the Sanskrit *trishula,* or trident, the three-pronged pike that crowns the temples of Shiva in India. Why Shiva, that dark, destructive member of the Hindu trinity? Then I recalled: Shiva was also god of the dance.

Religions and myths had followed us across Greek Macedonia and Thrace, from the city of the Thessalonians with its view of Olympus to the city of the old Philippians. Before crossing into Turkey, we camped on an Aegean beach with a superb view of the sunlit isle of Samothrace. We swam in the surf, and spread a feast on the sand. By lamplight, I leafed through St. Paul's letters and read his message to the Philippians, whose town we had passed that morning: "...I press on....forgetting what is behind me, and reaching out for that which lies ahead...."

Skopje rope vendor works as a family provider, a role Gypsy women often have filled as beggars and fortune-tellers.

$\mathcal{M}$ystic aura pervades Bulgaria's Rila
Monastery. A museum here contains treasures
that date as far back as the earliest
known presence of Gypsies in the Balkans
in the 14th century. Built by Turks, the

Tower of Skulls outside Niš, Yugoslavia,
displays the skulls of Serbian rebels. Gypsies,
held as slaves, saw the Ottomans occupy
Niš several times. A mourner in Skopje
seems to bear the sorrow of the ages.

Wild excitement reigns over a prenuptial rite in Skopje

as women of the groom's family scoop up henna to smear on the bride's hands

before wrapping them in cloth. The dye must stain the girl's skin

as a mark of piety. A Romany maxim that warns, "Shuk chi hal pe la royasa—

Beauty cannot be eaten with a spoon," supposedly guides the choice of Gypsy brides.

$\mathcal{B}$ridegroom Haidin Asip at 14 follows Romany custom by marrying

early. Gypsy families sometimes arrange betrothals of

much younger children. Marriage takes place after they

reach puberty. Revelers swirl to the bride's home for the

henna ceremony, and gather to feast outside the lighted Asip home.

*F*ather of the bride at first makes a noisy show of rejecting
a tribute of beer and brandy proffered by the groom's family,
but finally accepts it and releases the weeping
girl (right) for a wedding walk to her new home. In the spirit of
a Gypsy phrase, relatives present money along the way "to
give a push to the wheel of the new wagon."

*D*ressed in Balkan finery, a lad rides through Skopje's Gypsy
quarter before his ritual circumcision. Two others, one still in
the cradle, convalesce after the ceremony under their grandmother's
care in a room decorated for the occasion. Romany ingenuity and
fondness for extended celebration prompted the parents of
these two to schedule their circumcisions following a family wedding.

$\mathcal{C}$lifford Lee leads his wife Sheila and the

author down the Via Egnatia near Kaválla, Greece. His Gypsy ancestors

may have traveled this Roman highway almost nine centuries ago.

Another Gypsy rumbles over a modern road that crisscrosses the

ancient one above Kaválla. The isle of Thásos looms in the distance.

Greek Gypsy in his home village of Alexándria, near Salonica, demonstrates the Romany flair for entertaining with animals. Later, he tried to sell photographer Dale a trained monkey. From a barn door a child casts the kind of compelling gaze that moved Dale to call Gypsies "the most expressive people I've ever seen."

ike any other Greek yayá, *or grandmother, this old*
Gypsy of Flámbouron covers her head with a black scarf. Unlike others,
in the minds of some fellow villagers she holds the gifts of healing
or hexing as an ababina, *a sorceress. Most young people, however,*
doubt her powers. At right, painted carvings enliven a village doorway.

Bearded Karagöz, Gypsy star in old Turkish puppet plays, beguiles a lady.

Across the Bosporus into Asia

For our last few miles into Istanbul, we followed the Thracian route of the First Crusaders in 1096. "My people were a footnote on this footpath," Cliff said. Some historians speculate that Gypsies first entered Europe with returning Crusaders.

A highway sign proclaimed Istanbul, and beyond loomed the broken fortress wall of old Constantinople. In casual triumph we sped through its breach and into our last European city.

Here we had to regroup. We had been warned about the Asian miles ahead, the short supplies of gasoline, and the dangers of camping across Turkey. So we made repairs and took on fresh supplies.

Bruce had business back in Washington; he would fly home now and rejoin us in Iran. Since the campers needed service, we traded our sleeping bags for rooms at the Istanbul Hilton overlooking the busy water traffic of the Bosporus. And we picked up a large box of mail sent to us from Washington: itineraries, Gypsy lore, addresses of scholars in countries to the east.

In the covered bazaar I hunted heavy blankets for the chill mountain nights ahead, while Cliff and Sheila toured the jewelry shops. "I've never seen so much gold," Cliff mumbled. He bought one ring for about $10, then had the merchants appraise his Rumanian folly.

"It looks like 8-carat gold," one jeweler said. But his colleague applied the acid test to scrapings from the ring.

"Fake," he observed, "but a good fake." He looked shrewdly at Cliff. "*You'll* trade it easily." Cliff looked both hurt and flattered.

Professor Starkie had warned us that Turkey was "one of the countries where Gypsies seemed the lowest on the social scale."

"No doubt about it," said Dr. Mübeccel Kıray, a professor of sociology in Ankara. "Gypsies represent the lowest group in Turkey." The worst insult you can hurl at a Turk is to call him *Chingene* — Gypsy.

So we met a sampling of Turkey's estimated 70,000 Gypsies. Among the warehouses on the Golden Horn they worked as porters, wearing saddles on their backs like pack animals. On the streets we watched them shine shoes and sell flowers. And we visited the hive-like Gypsy neighborhoods of Çöplük (literally, "garbage-dump area") and Hacihüsrev, a hilly spot notorious for pickpockets. From three thick notebooks, a few individual Gypsies stand out:

Yavuz Tonton, 34, a resident of Lonca, a neighborhood of gifted musicians, had this to say: "I am a Gypsy, but I don't like the way Gypsies live here. My wife Sara is Jewish. Our families? Everyone was angry over our marriage. I have never met my wife's father. Some day I want to move to Canada."

A fortune-teller named Gülseren ("the rose spreader") Çekel talked shop. "I tell fortunes with palms or cards. Or I read beans in a kerchief. Some women read twigs or broken glass." Then she employed her best divining technique to read the sludge in my cup of Turkish coffee.

Veli ("good-hearted") Burgu was a young bear leader aged "14 or 15, I guess." His bear, a 4-year-old brown female named Necla ("yes, I know her age exactly"), had torn the ring from her nose the night before. Now she danced—dangerously—with only a dog collar as a restraint, while Veli shook a tambourine and sang sad love songs ("I have bloody tears in my eyes, and I am homesick for you..."). Necla wore bright ribbons, danced, and begged money from the Istanbul tourists. "I feed her only bread and fruit," said Veli, "for meat would cause rabies. Yes, I bought Necla three years ago already trained for 800 lira"—about $55.

My meeting Necla led us to a famous Gypsy bear trainer, Mr. Şahin Kuştepe, in a dim outskirt of Istanbul. "But don't call him 'Mister' " corrected our guide, a Tartar named Yılmaz Nogay. "We don't address Gypsies as 'Mister.' "

Şahin, a wizened and boozy man, carried a cub named Mehmis. We had heard that Gypsies trained cubs by making them stand on heated bricks; music is played while the bears lift their uncomfortable feet one at a time. Thus, Pavlov fashion, the bear associates music and "dancing" ever after. Did Şahin use this technique?

"No!" he insisted. "I use only the whip to train a cub." His conversation

Gypsy black tents, buffalo carts and decorated wagons, Romany words and smugglers mark the trek from Istanbul into old Armenia and on to Iran.

suddenly grew excited—and at last Yılmaz explained why: "I told him you were a circus owner and wanted to buy a bear. He asks 2,000 lira."

"A circus owner?" I said in some agitation. Şahin interrupted me.

"He saw your expression," said Yılmaz. "So he has reduced his price to 1,500 lira." That was about $100. We beat a swift retreat, "caught," as Cliff later remarked, "in a bear-faced lie."

In the old quarter of Balat, where Spanish Jews have lived since Ferdinand and Isabella expelled them in 1492, we lunched with Ibrahim Marangoz, a young Gypsy clarinetist.

"Every old neighborhood in Istanbul has Gypsies," he told us. "Now try one of our typical Rom foods—dried beans and meatballs in sauce." To this menu we added stuffed peppers, a sweet called "nightingale's nest," and "woman's navel"—meringue with a hole in it.

One evening our journalist friend Anne Turner Bruno showed us the colony of Sulukule ("tower with water"), built right into the old city walls of Constantinople. As early as the mid-1600's the Turkish historian Eremya Çelebi reported Gypsy ironmongers living here. Now a painted Gypsy girl named Gül was rippling through a belly dance, the traditional *göbek havasi*—clinking a rhythm with the *zil,* or finger cymbal.

"This area has long been famous for belly dancing," Anne told us. "The women here teach professional artists for a few lira a lesson."

"But today belly dancing has degenerated," said Dr. Metin And, ranking historian of Turkish theater and entertainment. "In the old days Gypsies greatly influenced the belly dance—and also the arts of conjuring and the jigging of puppets. The puppets are used in shadow plays, a one-man theater form perhaps brought here from India by Gypsies. Unfortunately, it's almost dead now...."

Dr. And showed us the jointed one-dimensional camel-leather puppets used here like Punch and Judy. The most famous, Karagöz, was a bearded rustic blacksmith—and probably a Gypsy. Attached to a stick, he was made to perform for audiences with a lamp behind him and a translucent screen in front.

"Gypsy words are used in the vocabulary of the Turkish theater," said

Dr. And. The words he mentioned sounded almost like the English Romany *pen* for speak, *churi* for knife, *dinilo* for stupid.

"More words, I wager," said Cliff, "than we got from the Turks."

Dr. And told us about one distant Anatolian village of Gypsy dancers who also begged ("they have even taught their donkeys to beg"), and of the way Gypsy women are hired to dance and serve food at peasant weddings. But his most extravagant stories concerned the *çengi,* the guild dancers of old Constantinople. Some 3,000 Gypsy boys danced in one guild alone, "all dressed in gold stuff," a 19th-century visitor reported.

Dr. And showed us one chronicle from the year 1582, when the Sultan Murat made "a great solemniti in the circumcising of . . . his Sonne." The "Solemne banquet lasted . . . seven whole dayes together." And when his food was cleared away, the Sultan "cast downe from his scaffolds, of golde and silver by handfuls . . . and . . . soone after the Sun was up, behold a great troupe and company . . . the Singers, Players of Instruments, Schollers, Monkes, Juglers, Tumblers, and Plaiers . . . some of them having theyr garmentes all . . . broken . . . other some halfe naked . . . and other some altogether naked and shameless without measure. Now these proper youthes . . . began to crie out, to snort . . . stryking uppon lyttle belles . . . with a moste straunge and confused noyse, entermixed with daunces, and theyr most horrible and dissolute behaviors. . . ."

Modern Sulukule seems moste straunge and even dissolute — but greatly changed.

"The whole settlement of 122 houses was destroyed by municipal authorities in 1966," explained Anne Bruno. "They warned the Gypsies to move because the walls were crumbling and there was danger of masonry collapsing onto the houses. But no one believed the authorities would tear down the huts. I was here the day after the bulldozers came. Gypsies weeping and standing in the ruins. Now you see how they have moved farther up the hill and across the road from the wall into newer but still shabby buildings."

"TEARING DOWN THE HUTS was not a police project," I was told at the Istanbul police department. "You see, there was very little crime there because that's where the honest musicians lived. The bad ones — the thieves and pickpockets — live elsewhere in the city."

For thousands of miles, I had skirted the question of Gypsy honesty. Now, while Cliff and Sheila were shopping, I asked candid questions of the hard men who police this corridor between Europe and Asia.

"Here in Istanbul," I asked, "are most Gypsies thieves?"

"No," said Yaşar Okçuoğlu, assistant director of the Istanbul police force. "Most Gypsies here are honest. And even the others do not commit large crimes — they lift wallets, but don't steal cars."

Would a Gypsy musician ever help a Gypsy pickpocket? "Oh, no," said Mr. Okçuoğlu, a bit shocked. "But perhaps you should see the chief of our pickpocket desk."

The dapper, meticulously barbered Mr. Zeki Arat presides over a staff of 40 detectives. "The police have registered the Gypsy pickpockets in two areas of Istanbul," he said. "Fewer than 600: 389 men, 141 women, 35 children under 11 years of age. Yes, the women stay pregnant, for under Turkish law pregnant women may not be jailed. And always a child works with a group. Let's say that a gang of six finds the *enayi,* the victim. The adults hold the man and take his wallet, then give it to the child. If they are caught, the child says, 'I did it,' and under the law the judge must turn him loose if he is younger than 11. Sometimes a Gypsy family waits three or four years to register a child's birth—that gives him a longer criminal career before he reaches age 11.

"I have met some very successful pickpockets—they owned cars, jewels, had apartments. They had been in the business 20 years. But I think our police make it harder today. Thieves now work outside our city jurisdiction. We have had no pickpocket case in Istanbul for two months. Of the some 10,000 Gypsies who live in the city, no more than perhaps 20 percent are involved in thievery. Gypsies are not so bad."

WE FELT READY FOR ASIA: provisioned, tuned, packed. I was sorting my notes for an early-morning departure when Sheila knocked on my door. Her face was tense and pale. "It's Clifford!" she said. "Come quick!" Only her Irish spunk held back the tears.

I found Cliff writhing in bed; pain had wrung the color from his face. "Terrible," he gasped. "Never such pain in my life—left side!" His body knotted forward and he seemed suddenly small and frail. He retched violently, then went limp.

"We're so far from home," he said to Sheila. "And now I'm leaving you this way." Obviously Cliff thought he was dying.

"Stay with him," I told Sheila and ran to a phone. In a moment I had the house of Dr. Warren Winkler, medical director of the Admiral Bristol Hospital. And in half an hour, Cliff was on his way to the hospital.

Not once did Sheila cry. But as we waited for news of the X-rays, she talked about Cliff's father. "He was 75 when they operated for gallstones," she said. "The operation didn't kill him, but he was literally frightened to death. . . . And Clifford's mother had never spent a night in any house—not until they took her to the hospital where she died." We speculated no further. But I quietly wondered whether our journey might end here.

A doctor interrupted our thoughts. "It's definitely a kidney stone," he said. "No—no surgery now. But he must stay here at least a few days."

Cliff himself, under heavy sedation, was too groggy for a celebration. Even Sheila and I still felt uncertain. Could we take Cliff straight from a hospital bed to the distant deserts and highlands of eastern Turkey, Iran, and Afghanistan? Would he even want to go on?

But Cliff's color returned next day along with his humor: "Yes, Istanbul is the only city where I've been stoned. . . . Can we call this a Cliff-hanger?" He refused, however, to eat any food from the hospital kitchen (*"Mulano!* Dismal!"), and the white sheets on the bed bothered him. "White's for mourning," he muttered.

And so we waited for new X-rays and the final release. When the time came, the doctor told Cliff, "You should be fine now, but another pain could recur any time." The hospital deputized me with an opiate and a hypodermic needle. But until Bruce joined us again, Cliff and I were the only drivers for our two cars—and I wondered what might happen if Cliff took sick again. Then we ran into a party of young British campers bound for India in a Land-Rover, Brian and Susan Douglas and their passenger Michael Spriggs.

"All three of us drive," said Brian. "And we can camp together for extra safety in eastern Turkey."

So, as we left, Dr. Winkler wished us well with two old Turkish sayings. The first seemed especially fitting for travelers—"*Yolunuz açık olsun,*" or "May your road be open." The second applies to all difficulties—"*Geçmiş olsun,*" or "May it pass easily." Especially apt for kidney stones.

The difficult Turkish language, related to languages of central Asia, frequently uses the passive voice, reflecting, perhaps, the Eastern origins of the Turks and their Oriental outlook. For us the language had a particular interest: Very few Turkish words can be found in European Romany. Why? Historians speculate that the Gypsies took no time to become close friends with the Turks.

Tribes of Turkoman nomads, shepherds mounted on camels and horses, began to push westward under the leadership of the Seljuk family, emerging from Khorāsān, which borders northwestern Afghanistan, after the year 1040. By 1071 a Turk leader named Alp Arslan had defeated and even captured the Byzantine Emperor in a battle at Manzikert on the eastern edge of Asia Minor. Within a generation the Seljuk Turks dominated Persia and most of the Asia Minor peninsula. Over its western reaches roamed wild Turkoman nomads.

Curiously, as the Seljuks advanced, taking slaves as part of the plunder, the Gypsies may have traveled westward just ahead of them, perhaps *because* of them. In any event, the Gypsies probably were moving about the same time from Khorāsān to the southern coast of the Caspian and then to old Armenia between the Caspian and Black Seas.

When the Turks attacked the Armenians during the latter half of the 11th century, many refugees fled south and then west as far as the Taurus Mountains along the Mediterranean. Gypsies might have accompanied these displaced persons. A surprising number of Armenian words, such as those for forehead and forge and horse, exist in all the European Gypsy dialects, indicating close contact over many years.

On their way to Jerusalem, the First Crusaders must have met Gypsies as they crossed the Taurus. Crusaders defeated the Turks in western Asia Minor, clearing the Byzantine roads for traffic to Constantinople. But 50 years later the Turks defeated the Second Crusaders in the same area. By the late 14th century, another tribe of Turks, the Ottomans, had taken control of most of the peninsula, had a European foothold on the Dardanelles, and threatened southeast Europe. The Ottoman Turks by 1380 ruled Macedonia, 73 years before they finally captured an isolated Constantinople. Dr. John Sampson explained the first Gypsy migration into western Europe in unqualified terms—the Gypsies were simply "terrified by the Turkish menace." No doubt, and hurried refugees would take no time to borrow words from the language of a foe.

Many Gypsies still roam Asia Minor. We met a fair sampling of them on our road to Ankara—dark, musical-comedy Gypsies traveling in barrel-top caravans pulled by horses or water buffalo. Near Düzce we stopped with a prosperous family of itinerant harvesters.

Istanbul shoeshiners, often Gypsies, attract customers with flashy brass, ornate polish bottles, and footstand art.

"Puzzling," said Cliff as he stroked the family kitten, "they call a cat *machka,* the way we do, and I thought that was a Hungarian word!" Actually, I learned, it comes from a Slavic source. Cliff could converse rather easily with these people, reminding us of Sampson's discovery that the Welsh Gypsies spoke in "a dialect hardly less pure than that of Paspati's" around Constantinople.

This was Sue Douglas's first brush with Gypsies, and while she warily watched the parents, some of the youngsters reached into her larder and stole a sack of onions. So we moved up the road to spend the night.

We camped, in fact, at a 2,800-foot elevation beneath a noble oak. Chill mountain air had gilded the outer leaves, so Cliff built a large fire, "the heart of any camp," he called it. And then we learned it was Brian's birthday, all the excuse Sheila needed to bake a Gypsy cake on the coals. Our gorgio companions unpacked a guitar and a fiddle, and music echoed through the woods. Then, mellow with food and song, Cliff began to talk about campfires, "but not some crow's nest of a fire that gorgios build inside stones. We Gypsies never put stones around our fire. It's not safe, since stones can break in the heat, cracking like rifle shots. A Gypsy can build a good fire even after a long rain. You look at the bottom of a hedgerow for dry bents — coarse grass — to start the blaze.

"Yes, fires attract everyone. In the early morning you see sleepy children come up to the fire rubbing their eyes as they wake up. And the dogs crawl out and stretch. And men hungry from tending the horses; they always bring back sticks for the fire. When a Gypsy is cold, he sits huddled up like a wet hen, but as the fire gets going, you can watch that Gypsy *expand.* Then the women come to cook. That's the reason Gypsy women wear long skirts. A modest way to sit around a fire.

"On a cold night, we used to build a broad fire, spread wide and low. Toward evening, we'd build a second one, but small, just to warm ourselves. Then we'd scrape all the embers from the ground and put our tent there. It'd be warm as anything. Wise old dogs on cold nights dig and turn around in the dead embers for a cozy bed. And if you have a bundle of money to hide, you can bury it, and build your fire over it. No, it won't burn up...."

IN ANKARA, the modern capital of Turkey, we called on some consulates for visas and road permits. While I played diplomat, Cliff prowled the Gypsy quarter of Cinçinkaya, where he reported a small discovery: "They call themselves *Rum,* instead of *Rom.*"

We heard the same term "Rum" — used by the Turks for the Byzantines — among wandering Gypsies on our road northeast to the Black Sea. Cliff found their Romany fairly easy to understand. For my part, I was dazzled by the brightly painted caravans — the most colorful we had seen on the entire trip.

Near Samsun we met the young family of Sali (the name means "laugh" in Romany) Toanausosi, camped in black tents and a barrel-top cart beside a gloomy graveyard. "We travel slowly," said Sali with a laugh, "for our three buffaloes are pregnant. For this reason I can't steal." He winked and held up his wrists as though they were cuffed, to show what would happen if he relied on a slow getaway cart.

Sali's mother served us tea in gold-trimmed cups — three cupfuls apiece.

BART McDOWELL, NATIONAL GEOGRAPHIC STAFF

Rainbow's end points to Asia across the Bosporus at Istanbul, showing the way east for the Gypsy hunters. Nearly a thousand miles later, they arrived at Doğubayazit, on the far Turkish horizon, close to Mount Ararat and Iran. There they had lunch beside a 200-year-old half-ruined palace and mosque.

Sali was the perfect host. He was 25, had three children, and held a regular laborer's job in the seaport of Samsun.

"I am on holiday," he said sadly, "and in one hour must start home. We are only true Gypsies now and then.... Do you have weapons? You need them—bad men ahead."

As we left, I pondered the warning, but Cliff was full of nostalgia: "They use *mandi* for 'me' and *lesti* for 'you' and 'him'—the way my family does. And they wished us *'Ja Develesa*—go with God.' Homely expressions."

We camped that night on a lonely Black Sea beach just outside a national forest. Next morning, out of nowhere, a pack of friendly youngsters emerged to watch us eat breakfast.

"At least we don't have to shave," said Cliff. "There's no photographer here to show how ugly we look." So we relaxed scruffily as we drove along the Black Sea coast. Bright green mountains crowded down to the water's edge, and youngsters sold figs beside the road.

One morning, a friendly farmer brought us a gift of fresh-caught fish. But somewhere along the route to the town of Trabzon, the road and the mood changed. Our way became pitted with potholes. We passed some ugly auto accidents. And then, in every eastern village, children pelted the car with stones. Once they even heaved a brick against Cliff's window.

"And I heard Clifford swear in English for the very first time," said Sheila in shocked awe.

Now we moved inland again toward the provincial capital of Erzurum, toiling upward through fern-covered hills that smelled of mint. Pokeberries were reddening, and thistles bloomed. Through a fog like skimmed milk, we negotiated Zigana Pass—named, some think, for Gypsies.

"This pass roughly marks the boundary of the old Armenian kingdom," Dr. Mübeccel Kıray had told me. Had bands of Gypsies fled through this gap to escape marauding Turks? Perhaps, for we know the Seljuk Turks pillaged and took slaves in this area. And more than death itself, Gypsies would have feared slavery.

Perhaps such speculation colored Cliff's reactions to eastern Turkey. We now traversed the wide Anatolian highlands. All Asia had suddenly opened up before us—dry, immense, hilly country with a blue sky of vast clarity. To the east, dominating the horizon for days, stood the icy grandeur of Büyük Ağrı Dağı, the Biblical Mount Ararat.

"Impressive scenery," said Cliff, "but the people are definitely xeno-phobic." So seemed the men who hurled rocks at us and tried to spit on us as we passed. Yet when we shopped for food in villages, or when we asked directions of the herdsmen, I always found the people polite and helpful. Only once did unpleasantness flare up at close range.

The place was Ağri, about 75 miles from the Iranian border. Our wind-swept campsites on the open highlands had been cold. (Sheila's dish-water, for example, froze in just 10 minutes.) Chilled and dirty, Michael and I stopped in Ağri at the *hamam,* or Turkish bath. Our friends waited outside while we thawed ourselves and shaved with the hospitable help of half the town. But when we emerged, a restless crowd of several dozen men was milling around the cars where Sheila and Susan were sitting.

"Let's get going quick!" said Cliff. "A policeman has already chased off this crowd once." It seemed that Susan's short skirt and unveiled face had brought out the local men to crowd around the cars and peer through the windows. We beat a retreat.

As soon as we were out of town, Cliff gathered a supply of stones. The next time villagers pelted him, he returned the favor.

THE WHITE CONE of Ararat seemed to grow as we approached the Iranian border. We picnicked near ruins of a 200-year-old palace and mosque and speculated about the old volcanic peak—a 16,946-foot anchorage for Noah's Ark. We recalled that some Sinti Gypsies of western Europe claim Noah as their ancestor. Once, their folktale claims, Noah got drunk and his son Caamo (Cham) mocked his father, who then "cursed him and said that he would be a slave; we remained slaves for a long time.... Half of our people, then, emigrated towards India.... others went in the opposite direction...."

For our own part we chose the east—but stopped after a few miles. Almost on top of the Iranian border we spotted three big black mohair tents in a Gypsy style. There we met Ahmet, a prosperous Gypsy smug-gler who owned a good transistor radio, a ballpoint pen (for his fluent signature), and an underwater wrist watch. Inside his tent we sat on warm sheepskin rugs for tea and the flat unleavened bread of eastern Turkey that we had come to enjoy.

Ahmet's daughters were brightly gowned with sequin-trimmed scarfs. "But no pictures," our host insisted. His objection was more than re-ligious; he himself would not pose with any outdoor landmark, a proper precaution for a smuggler.

We had been warned to pack pistols into the wilds of eastern Turkey. "You'll meet dangerous outlaws," people had predicted. Ahmet the smug-gler was undoubtedly an outlaw; perhaps he was even dangerous. But he was also a gracious host. So, with somewhat muddled ethics, we now omit all incriminating details of his calling—but only to protect the guilty.

Finger cymbals go chik-a-chik-a-chik, *as a Gypsy belly dancer casts her spell in Casino D'Istanbul.*

*Circling and laughing with belly dancers
in a restaurant near Istanbul lead to a vibrant solo
on a chair seat — and a chance for patrons to tuck
money, politely, into some corner of the
performer's costume. Girls of the Gypsy Sulukule
quarter begin learning the rippling movements
of the belly dance as soon as they can walk.*

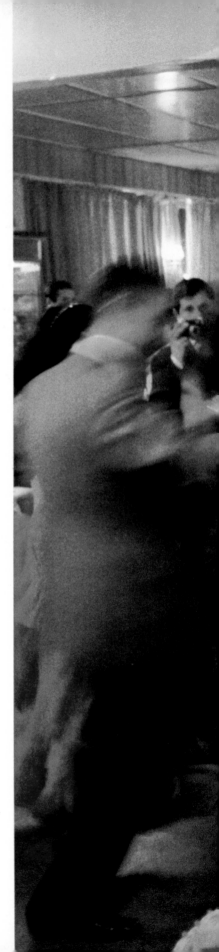

BRUCE DALE (ABOVE AND OVERLEAF) AND YILMAZ NOGAY

"*F*eels great," *Bruce Dale sighs as 200 gentle pounds of*
bear press the kinks out of his back. When Cevriye finished the 10-lira (70-cent)
massage, she sat down. Her trainer then jokingly asked 20 lira, Dale said,
"to get the beast off my back." Children race to windows (above)
and into streets when bear leader Ismet bangs his tambourine (overleaf)
and calls, "Come on, my girl, dance. Show your friends a little twist."

Persian artist signs his whimsical creation on the door of the party's Volkswagen.

Cold Camps and Gypsy-killer Pass

WHEN a wandering Gypsy wants to leave a message for those following him, he arranges twigs on the roadside in some agreed fashion. This signal he calls a *patrin*—literally, a leaf. Now in Iran—the very name means "Land of the Aryans"—a variety of patrins made our ancient Gypsy trail uncertain. A particularly alluring one is found in the shimmering poetry of old Persia. We turned to the *Shahnameh,* or Book of Kings, written ten centuries ago.

In this book the great poet Firdawsi sings of Bahram Gur, the hunter Shah who ruled Persia in the fifth century from his capital near Baghdad. His poor subjects complained that they went hungry and ate mud while the rich wore wreaths of flowers and drank wine in the company of musicians. The Shah "laughed much" and sent word to Shangol of India to send him harpists—"...Luris...ten thousand, male and female... riding on ducks"—a joking reference to that tribe's known love for stealing fowl. When the minstrels arrived, Bahram Gur gave each an ox and an ass and some wheat, proposing to make them farmers. But they ate the cows and the wheat, and so the Shah ordered them "to go forth and play music to make the people happy as though they were in silk. And now the

Luris, according to his word, wander all over the world, having wolves and dogs for neighbors and fellow travelers, stealing nights and roaming during the day."

Variations of the same story appear in other documents, before and after Firdawsi, with the wanderers variously identified as Luri, Luli, and Zott. Scholars say Zott is the way Arabs pronounced the Indian tribal name "Jat," and the name they gave anybody from the Indus Valley.

And there are other patrins: Some historians, for example, tell of Zott-Jat war prisoners brought with their water buffalo from the Indus Valley to the head of the Persian Gulf in the eighth century. They became high-way robbers so strong and terrible it took an army to defeat them.

Thus the patrins of poet and historian pointed south toward the lands of old Persia. Our route lay through Azerbaijan Province, where we kept a rendezvous with Bruce in Tabriz.

But there we found that the local Gypsies had already fled south to escape the chilly weather, so we too headed toward warmer climes, passing camel caravans and extravagantly costumed wanderers. The people had a familiar walk. They moved, in fact, the way British portraitist Augustus John described two Gypsy girls, striding "aloof and enigmatic, like nuns of some unknown and brilliant order."

"If we stayed here a long time," said Cliff, "we must have learned things — how to walk long distances, how to fold bedding. . . ."

And words. While here in Iran, Cliff's forebears quite possibly split into two bands, giving rise to two dialects: the European Romany of those who passed to the north through Armenia, and the fragmentary dialect of those traveling south to Syria. In Persia they borrowed many words, among them ones for wool, silk, and — probably after seeing the Caspian — ocean. Just as English-speaking people indirectly adopted the word "magic" from the Persians, so Romany was enriched by *baht* — meaning luck or fortune. "And maybe the Persians taught us *dukkeripen* — fortune-telling" — Cliff suggested.

Iranian Gypsies use palms and beans and even the knuckle bones of sheep to foretell the future. "Our people in Britain read palms and crystal balls and sometimes an egg white in a glass of water," said Cliff over the campfire one night. "But I wager they say the same things. As a boy, I'd hide under the bed in our caravan and listen for hours to my mother telling fortunes: 'You're born to be lucky in some things but not all. You have a friend who isn't a friend — beware! Have you had a letter that has come across water? Well, you *will* quite soon.' And one thing that's always good: 'You've helped others who wouldn't help you.' They talk for hours about ingratitude! It helps to know human nature — and maybe something about your client."

My thoughts reached back to Epsom on Derby Day. "Cliff," I asked, "do you know an English fortune-teller named Madam Thorney?"

"You mean Thorney Lee. Of course. Probably a kinswoman," said Cliff. And would she have known about our trip before we left? "I'd guess every Gypsy in England could have heard about it," said Cliff. So I had gone to Epsom with my American accent, my camera, my notebook. Maybe her prediction of our journey was not too surprising after all.

Yet Cliff Lee's family has long been famous for fortune-telling. Professor Starkie tells how Cliff's Grandmother Lee foretold "to the very

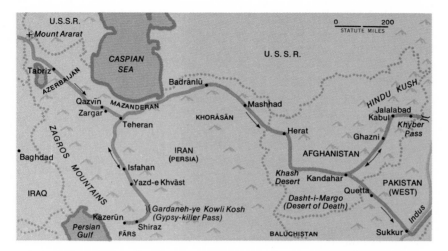

From Turkey an increasingly dusty road plunges into Iran and Afghanistan, mysterious lands of arid steppes, craggy horizons, and ancient Persian poetry.

month the ridiculous death of my aunt—she got out of an automobile on the wrong side, was struck by a boy on a bicycle, and never regained consciousness." And Dr. Yates even tells how Cliff himself once foretold the abrupt marriage of a 65-year-old maiden lady.

"But I didn't do it for money, mind you," Cliff adds, embarrassed. "I guess there are things about dukkeripen that we cannot explain."

In Teheran, we took on reinforcements, Donald and Sharon Stilo. Don was a young American linguist working on his doctorate and interested in Romany. But he had never camped overnight anywhere, and our route to Shiraz near the Persian Gulf would take us through some remote country, including one mountain pass called Gardaneh-ye Kowli Kosh.

"That means Kowli-killer Pass," said Don. "Kowli is one name for Gypsy." Other names for the Iranian Gypsies—their number is unknown —are: Juki; Karachi or "black" in Turkish; Qorbati or "alien" in Arabic.

In deference to our tenderfoot linguist, we spent our first night in Isfahan in a dazzling new hotel. Then, barely taking time to marvel at the mosaic splendor of the Royal Mosque, we moved on south. Soon the whole earth seemed hostile. On the horizon, peaks of the Zagros Mountains tilted sharp and steep like waves in a stormy sea. No plant stood taller than knee-high, and restless tan whirlwinds drilled into the dry land.

About a hundred miles south of Isfahan at a town called Yazd-e Khvāst—"wanted by God," as Don translated—we asked a truck driver directions. "Straight ahead," he told us. And why was the pass called the Gypsy-killer? "It kills everyone. Ten to 14 feet of snow every winter. Long ago, many Kowlis died there. Then no one had cars, only camels and donkeys. They slipped and fell. And died."

From this traditional description I was expecting a precipitous drop. Instead, by twilight, we found bare slopes with tufts of sagebrush and nettle. Bruce's altimeter read 2,400 meters—about 7,500 feet.

It occurred to me that Gypsy-killer Pass would be the psychological spot for Cliff to have another attack of kidney stones. I even readied my needle. Instead, as the wind rose to a thin whine, Cliff turned up his lantern and quietly read himself to gentle sleep with Omar Khayyam.

We referred next day to the Persian poet Hafez in Shiraz, capital of the Province of Fārs, or Parsa, from which Persia took its name. "Shiraz, city of the heart," the pleasure-loving Hafez called it. And among its charms were the Gypsy girls, "these saucy Lulis, dear beguilers...."

But the Gypsies we met in the Bibidokhtar section of Shiraz were unbeguiling. The men carved mouthpieces for flutes and hubble-bubble pipes, and their families lived in squalor.

"Gypsies, called Qorbati or Kowli here, often attach themselves as smiths or tinkers or peddlers to the various tribes of the nomadic Kashgai confederacy," we were told by the distinguished educator Mohammad Bahmanbegui, himself a Kashgai. "Right now my people with their sheep and goats are moving from the Zagros Mountains down to winter pastures below Kāzerūn, a journey of two to three hundred miles."

So we decided to follow some of the 150,000 Kashgai and their camels, donkeys, horses, and flocks.

Our road out of Shiraz led through magnificently sculptured mountains and into broad grassy valleys. In a single panorama of Biblical sweep we counted 22 campsites of black Kashgai tents—perhaps 200 families to the camp—with dark clumps of distant grazing flocks.

The country bleached white and dry near the Persian Gulf, and my notebook filled with oddments—"We navigate sea of black goats.... Pass a boy who holds up his goatskin and implores, 'Āb! Water!' We share.... Pass herdsmen, even their eyelashes powdered with dust...."

We camped among the Kashgai one night. They had been on the road 40 days—and "we have 15 more to go," said one shepherd. "I must make these shoes last the trip." His toes peeked out the sides.

DON QUOTED US an old Persian saying: "By asking and asking, you can even arrive at Mecca." The next day we asked and asked—and finally found a black-tent colony of five families of Qorbati ironsmiths. The nomads look down on them, but the Qorbati men wear Kashgai felt hats with wide turned-up flaps because they have formally put themselves under tribal rule. Using a goatskin bellows and sturdy hammers, two smiths at an open-air forge were whanging away on red-hot metal—"old car springs," Bruce noticed.

"Yes, we make hammers and saws to sell," said our host, Mehrab Haddadi, in his south Persian dialect; he denied speaking Romany or any other private language. "In the season of rain, we cannot work at the forge. So for three months we make felt tents."

An old woman brewed tea, setting the china pot directly on the coals beside the bellows. We shared the family's one spoon. Later I asked Cliff's impressions. "These Qorbatis look and act like Gypsies," he said. "And yet I just don't *regard* them as Gypsies."

In Kāzerūn, about 50 miles west of Shiraz, Cliff reacted differently to some Qorbati flute makers. Even before he spoke to them, Cliff told me, "These may be!" Sheila glanced my way when the old woman washed her hands before fixing tea. "Like Romanichals," she said.

Don found the language strange: "All the numerals are Persian—with Armenian endings." But a hasty survey turned up several words—those for brother, hungry, sheep—obviously related to European Romany. They all come from Sanskrit. Later the Qorbatis told Don of three Gypsy dialects spoken in the area: pastoral, ironsmith, and coppersmith.

"Then you are Rom!" whooped Cliff.

"What is 'Rom'?" asked the old man. Thus far, none of the Gypsies we had met in Iran had ever heard the word—or the Turkish Gypsies' "Rum."

"Cultural amnesia," Cliff grumbled.

As we headed north to pick up a patrin that pointed due east, we pondered a question that has long haunted scholars: What is the relationship between Gypsies in Iran and those in Europe? Are the Qorbatis and Kowlis descended from Cliff's forebears—or from brother countrymen of an earlier period and a different part of the Indus Valley, or a combination of both?

As if to underscore the difficulty of unscrambling origins, Don Stilo directed us to some "round-trip" Gypsies, near Qazvīn, 90 miles northwest of Teheran, who call themselves "Romi."

These are Gypsies who came back from Europe generations ago and finally settled here as farmers, Don told us. We visited them in the mud-sculptured village of Zargar—"goldsmith" in Persian—a place that resembled a Pueblo Indian community.

Don had a hand in Zargar's linguistic discovery in 1968. While here on a project with Professor Gernot L. Windfuhr of the University of Michigan, Don identified this baffling language as European Romany. Now he introduced us to some of the 450 watermelon farmers there.

"We lived in tents until 40 or 50 years ago," said Ghodrat Ramazan Zargar, the gray village elder. "But our people came long ago. Three brothers, goldsmiths, were brought by Nader Shah,"—a colorful 18th-century ruler of Iran—"who gave them exemption from taxes and military duty. I saw the Shah's own charter, but it was burned some years ago by the wife of our headman. The woman went crazy and threw the Shah's charter into her oven."

The oven gets tastier use today, as we discovered when the Zargaris spread a feast for us upon the floor of the headman's house. While Cliff excitedly compared dozens of Romany words with almost identical ones of our hosts, Ghodrat played music on his *chavora* flute. To its humming, reedy sound, a boy danced the *halay,* "like a Scottish reel," noted Sheila.

In the first scholarly paper ever written about Zargar, Professor Windfuhr has described the language of these farmers "as a Romany dialect from the Balkans." As he explains it, "Although heavily under the influence of their present Turkish-speaking neighbors, the Zargaris speak a language that has the same Greek words as Romany dialects in the Balkans. It seems to include even some Hungarian words—but I like to leave the final localization of Zargari to the Gypsiologists." Fine. And when those scholars come to Zargar, let them be warned: One woman successfully monged—begged—the scarf off my neck, and two knives that we had lent our hosts got spirited away.

Heavy clouds were gathering—appropriately, since this was the first day of *Ābān,* the month that usually provides water. We hurried to beat the storm. And, sure enough, after we said goodbye to the Stilos and Teheran, we drove through rain for days. We followed Caspian beaches —"like the North Sea on a wet Sunday," said Cliff—and well-watered

"Half conversation, half charade," said the author as he watched Cliff Lee converse. Lee found he could communicate with most Gypsies from England to India.

forests with palms and bamboo. Here in Mazanderan Province, says John Sampson, the Gypsies borrowed the word *vesh,* meaning "forest" or "wood." Then, abruptly, we returned to a dry world, some of the bumpiest, dustiest roads of our trip—and to cold campsites.

My logbook shows the spidery writing of chilled fingers: "Camp near farmhouse. 30 mph wind. Bedding inventory: sleeping bag, 2 goat-hair blankets, one camel-hair blanket, one newspaper *(The Times* of London). Morning: cirrus clouds. Valley vast as all Asia—no foreground, no middle distance. Only mountainous background and dusty tumbleweeds."

We had reached old Khorāsān, a land traversed by Cliff's people about a thousand years ago. In the first half of the 11th century, the Ghaznavid rulers defended these dry steppes against nomadic Seljuk Turks plundering from the north. The Turks finally won because, complained one Ghaznavid courtier, "the steppe is father and mother to them, just as towns are to us." A warrior observed, "Their camels can forage freely . . . they have no heavy baggage. . . ."

So the Seljuk Turks and their close-cropping sheep "devoured [Khorāsān]," as the scribe Baihaqī said of earlier Turks, "as if it were food laid out for hunting falcons." And any Gypsies wandering there at the time must have fled westward.

The people of Khorāsān—mostly Turkomans, transplanted Kurds, Afghans—were as friendly as any on our trip. "Of all the countries we've seen, I'd most like to live in Iran," said Sheila. "The people are so gentle."

Even in Mashhad, capital of Khorāsān and holiest city in Iran, we found surprising hospitality toward Westerners. Near the glittering dome of the Golden Mosque we met Javad Habary, son of Kowli carpet weavers and a student at the University of Mashhad. He showed us the city. On one corner we passed a gorgio fortune-teller whose caged goldfinch plucked up a slip of paper in its bill. Javad read it.

"I will marry a beautiful young lady." He laughed. "I don't believe these things. Gypsies here read palms." Then he talked about his life as a Kowli boy, about weddings and camels and carpet weaving, and how a grade-school teacher had influenced him to become a scholar. "At school, people asked about my father's job. I was ashamed that he had none. People feel a Kowli is low. Yet I was accepted by five universities."

At the Afghan border we met a curious compound of the old and new. The highway, built by Russians in the late 1950's, was the best we had seen on the whole trip. But customs took three hours while gravely polite men in karakul hats scribbled tirelessly with steel dip pens.

The city of Herat continued on the same split-level time zone. This 2,770-year-old oasis had a hotel so new that no one had yet discovered how to cash traveler's checks.

Our own discoveries were even more difficult. We fruitlessly inquired about a number of Gypsy-like people—Toryans (fortune-tellers and monkey trainers), Jats (peddlers, drum makers, and medical bleeders), Masalyan and Lotyans (musicians), and Alish-badalan (animal traders).

So we moved down the highway. Since our road ran through Khash Desert and along the edge of Dasht-i-Margo, the dread Desert of Death, we preferred night travel. Thus we viewed the mud houses of Afghan villages, windows flickering orange from oil lamps like great jack-o'-lanterns.

Our headlights scanned a sandy, mortal flatness. Gradually hills grew up around us. Daylight revealed a craggy horizon of wild stone peaks, and the ruins of old caravansaries at 12-mile intervals—each a camel-day of travel. We met little traffic except for magnificent trucks decorated with lurid murals in the style of a tattoo parlor: panels showing South Sea islands, the Taj Mahal, galleons under sail, peacocks.

Beyond Kandahar at a village called Maranjan, we came upon a wedding procession with the veiled bride riding a chestnut horse. A bevy of girl musicians—barefaced, rouged, and draped with bright ornaments— beat on *daira,* half-drums, and sang. We stopped.

"Jat," affirmed one old villager. These were Jat entertainers here to assist villagers. I wanted to record the music, but brides are especially vulnerable to the evil eye, and the local chaperones waved us on by chucking some good-sized rocks.

I N KABUL we continued our pursuit of the Jat set, as Cliff called them. "There's snow on the Hindu Kush," said Abdul Haq Waleh, editor of the newspaper *Caravan.* "So the Jats should be going to Jalalabad, near the Khyber Pass. It's 80 miles down the canyon."

With Waleh—his pen name—as a volunteer guide, we followed the Jats toward the Pakistan border. Since 1961 this Khyber Pass entry has been closed to nomads by the Pakistani government. But Jats still slip across, sometimes smuggling gold molded into temporary teeth.

We found wild mynahs that day and balmy breezes scented with oleander—but no Jats. Yet the drive was worth it. This chasm had been a main route for all the great conquerors of Asia. Through this gorge came the war elephants of the Sultan Mahmud of Ghazni; early in the 11th century he built a great Afghan-Persian empire and sent 17 predatory war expeditions into India. The remarkably ugly Mahmud, a cultured if ruthless conqueror, even took a captive scientist-historian, Albiruni, along as a war correspondent; and the sultan's court counted 400 poets.

"So we know much about Mahmud," said Waleh. "We even know about his swarthy slave Ayaz, who was a shrewd judge of jewels and horses."

"Could this Ayaz have been a Gypsy?" Cliff asked. The notion seemed possible, since Mahmud brought back vast numbers of Indian slaves — the forebears of our own Gypsies, some scholars believe.

In Kabul again, we called on Dr. Rawan Farhadi, then Director General of Political Affairs, now Deputy Foreign Minister.

"No, our Gypsies have never been properly studied," he told us in his office at the Ministry for Foreign Affairs. But he discussed some vivid details about groups like the Jats: "The Jat women are very manly — they are never veiled and visit our countrywomen selling needles, pins, and glass bangles, reading palms, and extracting blood from the sick. Men work at home — making drums and tambourines, for example; they also cook and care for the children. Each day one man in the Jat community announces the menu — 'Today we are having *kichri qorut.'* (That's rice with dried salted yogurt.) Then all the Jats in the clan eat the same food that day."

We asked whether any people here called themselves Rom. "Never," said Dr. Farhadi. "Not east of Anatolia. The word 'Rom' has several meanings — Rome, the city and empire, and also the Eastern or Byzantine Empire — and thus to us it means Anatolia. In North Africa, 'Rumi' means European or Christian. And in Iran and here in Afghanistan, 'Rom' means 'western,' or vaguely in the direction of Turkey. Gypsies first encountered the name 'Rom' when they reached Asia Minor.

"How have Gypsies kept their sense of unity? *An Indian sense of caste!* They took their caste system all the way to Europe."

From the Foreign Ministry, we made a swift social descent to the home of a Jat sieve maker. He greeted us hospitably, showed us his sieves, served us tea, and talked while wiping his nose on the tail of his turban. His words seemed utterly foreign to Cliff's Romany, and his gentle manner lacked the flashing, mercurial quality of Gypsies. But just outside his house stood one dark, quick boy about ten.

"Him? Not a Jat at all — a Churiwala," said our host. "His family trains monkeys." So we followed the dark boy home to a wild encampment of tents nearby. Monkeys were tethered beside every campfire — at least a hundred of them. As we passed, monkeys screeched and danced, dogs barked, and black-eyed girls waved arms adorned with jingling bangles.

One family was packing for a seven-day migration on horseback to Jalalabad, but another had chartered a truck — one embellished with paintings of ships, ducks on the wing, the Sphinx, and Washington, D. C.'s Jefferson Memorial. Onto this truck men were loading blankets, kerosene lamps, kettles, children, and monkeys.

Sheila Lee shops in Mashhad, Iran, for nān, *an unleavened bread with a nutty flavor, baked from rough-milled flour.*

"I thought monkey trainers were called Toryans," I said. Our hosts looked embarrassed: I quickly learned that Toryan is an impolite word meaning "blackie."

Churiwala here means bangle-seller, even though Cliff insisted *"churi* ought to mean knife." Yet that day I jotted down at least 50 Churiwala words that seemed close to Romany.

Briefly in Kabul we took time to shop, then bought camel-hide luggage to hold our purchases. The handle came off my bag on the first heft, and, once loaded, both cars soon began to smell like an Oriental tannery. "Sorry," said the hard-faced dealer when we returned. "Purchase is final." Cliff muttered, then shrugged with good grace. So we tied our redolent bags onto the luggage rack—in the open air.

In Ghazni, below a honeycombed mountain fortress, we kept a rendezvous with the Sultan Mahmud. Upon a hillside that the conqueror himself chose, he rests within an inscribed alabaster sarcophagus.

Afghans were burning incense when we stopped. Families came, the women piously veiled, paid prayerful respect, and left without speaking.

They honored a man who came to power here in A.D. 997, and who during a 30-year period pushed his domain outward in all directions. Such a conqueror's conqueror was he that in ten tormented centuries no invader ever dared despoil Mahmud's grave. So, in his posthumous presence, we reviewed Mahmud's reputed part in the history of our Romanies.

As an example, we examined his Indian campaign of the year 1025

when "the Jats...molested his army," as a chronicler reported. The Sultan resolved to punish the Jats, and the next year he "led a large force toward Multan." There he launched a fleet of 1,400 armed boats: "In each boat were twenty archers, with bows and arrows, grenades, and naphtha; and in this way they proceeded to attack the Játs...." The Jats launched an opposing fleet, but "Every boat of the Játs... was broken and overturned.... The Sultán's army proceeded to the places where their families were concealed, and took them all prisoners. The Sultán then returned victorious to Ghaznín."

So those Jats—like tens of thousands of other swarthy slaves brought out of northwest India—bent their backs in Mahmud's service. But the ugly old Sultan died, and soon his son Mas'ud had lost both a war and an empire to the Seljuk Turks.

Thus the old Gypsy trail seemed to cross some Turkish tracks here. Did the Turks take over Mahmud's slaves as booty? Or, in the confusion of war, did bands of Indian slaves escape toward the west? But why, we wondered, would they not return to Mother India?

Obviously, unfinished business was waiting for us in Pakistan and India. What about those similar names—the Sindi of the Indus and Sinti of the Rhine, the Dom of India and the Rom of Europe? These questions have intrigued many a scholar and linguist.

We replaced four broken shock absorbers, and started south. But something seemed to be missing.

"Your ring," I asked Cliff—"where's your Rumanian folly?"

"I traded," Cliff said, smiling. "For these karakul furs." He pointed to a pile of lush pelts. "The ring must have really been gold—or that's what our friendly leather dealer thought. And, of course, we all know his policy—purchase is final."

Kufic Arabic inscription marks the tomb of 11th-century Sultan Mahmud of Ghazni; some Gypsies may have descended from his Indian slaves. Opposite, a flute maker's daughter in Kāzerūn nuzzles a pet dove.

$\mathcal{L}$aden with sacks of grain and rugs for tent floors,

donkeys belonging to Iranian Gypsies, or Qorbatis, plod a dusty

road near Shiraz. Qorbatis often attach themselves to tribes of

nomadic Kashgai herdsmen — and copy their dress. The bejeweled

Qorbati woman at right looks much like her hosts, who annually

drive flocks of sheep and goats between mountain and lowland

pastures. Outside his open-front tent a Qorbati ironsmith sharpens

a farrier's knife he has just made for sale to the Kashgai.

$\mathcal{L}$owering clouds beyond a young shepherd herald Ābān—the rainy month—

at Zargar, Iran. Generations ago, the ancestors of Zargar's Gypsies

migrated to Europe. Brought back as goldsmiths in the 18th century, most

eventually became farmers. The author's host (left) cradles his daughter: a wide-angle

lens slightly distorts sloping walls of mud-brick homes (opposite upper).

Bright lantern flame lights a feast of welcome at Zargar held for Bruce Dale (at right) and visiting American linguist Donald Stilo (beside Dale). In 1968 Stilo helped identify the Zargari language as European Romany. Dishes included lamb, fowl, rice, and bread. A sheet serves as a tablecloth, protecting a Persian carpet.

Agile Kashgai jump and whirl as they perform a stick dance — like those of Balkan Gypsies — at a wedding near Shiraz. Drums and horns sound the rhythm as one dancer armed with a stick tries to whack the legs of another.

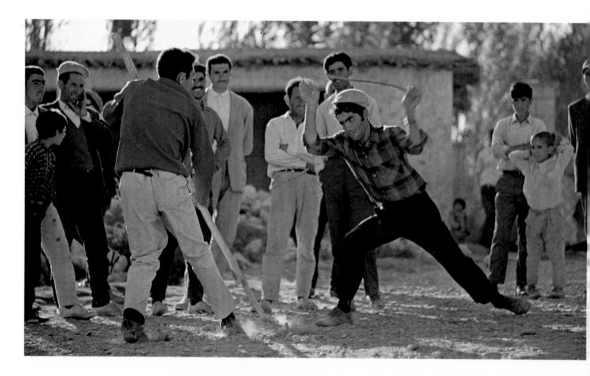

*D*un-colored village of
Badrānlū huddles beneath barren slopes in
northeastern Iran. Cold campsites and
gusty winds plagued the author's party during
much of their journey in this region.
Near the Persian Gulf, desolate solitude
surrounds them (opposite below) as they
camp on a near-desert outside Kāzerūn. Below,
a silvery road linking Shiraz and Isfahan
passes through the Zagros Mountains.

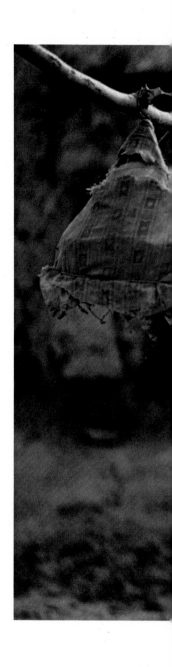

*P*et mynah perched on his head, a Jat hangs fighting quail,
covered to keep them quiet, on a branch near Kabul, Afghanistan.
Nearby, in a Churiwala camp, a monkey clambers over its
trainer's wagon; a young girl plays on a rubble-strewn lot.

Tiny Iranian toddler sips the juice
of a melon steadied by her mother.
Luminous eyes of a Jat girl in Kabul
(below) complement silver coins and baubles.
Nearer India, Gypsies become more and more
difficult to identify among dark-skinned,
dark-eyed gorgio neighbors in colorful dress.

Reed-veiled Sukkur rises beside the Indus, the river that gave its name to a subcontinent.

The Mystery Remains Intact

MUSIC LED US down into Pakistan. On our car radio the volume rose and fell as we twined through the dry, fortified mountains on the frontier: odd music with vocals that ranged from falsetto to veiled bass. The Persian poet Hafez had described "those soft-voiced Lulis" of Shiraz; now Radio Pakistan identified their staff minstrels as Luris. We had returned to the epic tale of Firdawsi, his hunter Shah, and the minstrels.

So our first appointment in flower-garnished Quetta was at the Radio Pakistan studios.

"Luris prefer not to be called Luris," warned the regional director, Ahmad Bushir. "Our most popular singer here is Fez Mahomed—but he calls himself a minstrel—a Pahlwan—or a Dom. The Luri stands at the very bottom of the social scale. And yet he has a certain security: If a man harms a child, a woman—or a Luri—he is scorned."

Luris were never thieves, beggars, or prostitutes. "And Luri women are often light of skin and are famous for their beauty," added Hadji Abdul Qaiyum, President of the Baluchi Academy. "The Luris' dialect is like a code. They say some words backward to confuse outsiders."

Mr. Qaiyum told us about "my own Luri," as he called a man in his home village. "He has certain reserved jobs that are his right in my family: to perform circumcisions, to sharpen knives, to dress the bridegroom at weddings, and so on. Even if the wedding is held elsewhere, and someone else does the work, I must still pay my Luri for the job.

"At social gatherings, Luris amuse the people, telling anecdotes, making everyone laugh. They also arrange marriages in big families, for they hear gossip about the young people and know who is good. Luris are honest and very faithful to the families they are attached to, and it is their cherished desire to bring into the family wives of repute.

"Most of the good Baluchi poets are Luris. They are also good musicians and singers. Yet, even though I do not approve of the caste system, I would not give my daughter to a Luri, because Luris are still socially and economically backward."

One of the leading young poets of Pakistan, Ata Mohammad Shad, comes from the same group. "Yes, I have a children's radio program here —as Uncle Kabben Kaka," he told us at the studios. He is a sinewy young man—"age 29, or so I suppose," he told us. "A grade-school teacher once estimated my age." Mr. Shad has composed more than 4,000 songs, some of which we heard when Fez Mahomed brought his ensemble of Luris or Doms to play and sing for us. The music reminded me of Spanish flamenco with a touch of Turkey.

"I come from Baluchistan," Fez Mahomed told me later, through Mr. Shad's translation. "That is, the Iranian part of Baluchistan. But I had relatives working in Karachi as coolies on the dock. So I went there to do the same, carrying burdens on my back with a saddle—and singing for weddings when I could. And I also sang while I worked on the dock. Or I did until my boss came to me one day and gave me five rupees. 'Don't sing,' he said. 'Men leave their work to listen.' " Thus began a career that has made Fez Mahomed an idol throughout Pakistan.

Mr. Shad introduced us to less fortunate Luris in Quetta's slums— scrap-metal scavengers and tinkers. "And many Luris still live a roving life," he told us.

So, with Mr. Qaiyum accompanying us, we joined the seasonal route of the Luris of western Pakistan, heading for the famous Bolan Pass, a mountain corridor used for tens of centuries by peaceful nomads with their camels and donkeys.

The Bolan Pass stands bare, dry, hard, and 60 miles long. To me it resembles a cave turned inside out. Precipitous walls close in on the narrow road; then the passage widens into a broad wasteland where boulders wildly strew a riverbed that is waterless over much of its length.

We watched camel-borne Brahui nomads pass through the canyon and the stony wastes beyond. Each family here would travel 15 to 20 miles a day. "And each has one or two Luris along," said Mr. Qaiyum. "They travel in winter to avoid the heat. Summer temperatures reach 120° Fahrenheit, and at night no one can sleep."

We had no such trouble when we stayed in an attractive government cottage near Sibi. Then, trying to beat the heat ourselves in this sahara—

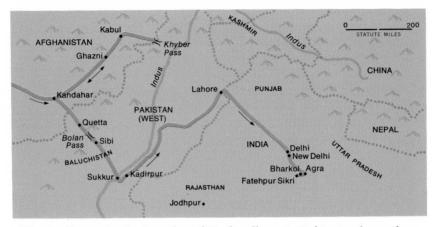

After leading to Luri minstrels and Sindi villages in Pakistan, the trail comes to an end with a flight to New Delhi in the Indian homeland of the Gypsies.

five inches of yearly rainfall—we bade our host goodbye and took to the road at dawn. The temperature reached 94° by 9 a.m.—the hottest weather Cliff and Sheila had ever endured. Mirages washed away the flat horizon. Thus, as buttes receded behind us, we crossed a country of thornbush and sand. By 11 a.m., we noticed that most nomads had halted for the day. We joined them to talk about camel prices (from 400 to 2,000 rupees each—$84 to $420) and to watch their dogs hug the shadows of the camels. Then we moved on across the desert toward the Indus.

We reached it, the river that gave its name to this subcontinent, at the cluttered city of Sukkur. There we crossed its waters by a formidable causeway, and lunched on the eastern bank. Now we had arrived in the old land of Sind, conquered by Mahmud in 1006.

"In Europe, I found Sinti Gypsies the most like my people," Cliff remarked. "Now I want to compare them with the Sindi."

We had ample chance. We went into all sorts of alluvial backlands along the Indus looking for good picture possibilities. Darkness caught us one evening near the village of Kādirpur, about 20 miles north of Sukkur, and we asked the local chairman for permission to camp.

"You are our guests," said Hadji Mir Ghulan Mustafa. He spoke slowly and bowed just as slowly, a huge, cumulous man with kingly hospitality.

Foreign visitors are rare in Kādirpur, so some 1,500 male residents turned out to greet us. Under the chairman's banyan tree, we took tea by lamplight. Villagers approached, touched our host's hand in tribute, then sat cross-legged around us. When the chairman addressed any villager, the local man respectfully rose before answering. Cliff tried out some Romany words with only fair success. "And the local Sindi expressions aren't like anything I've ever known," he added.

No villager here had ever heard of European Gypsies—or even of Pakistani Luris, 250 miles away. One man asked Bruce, "Is it really true the Americans sent men to the moon? It seemed too far away."

As the hour grew late, two *dhol*—kettle-like drums—suddenly began to sound and a man and his son started to dance in the dust. We watched the gyrations, the exaggerated facial expressions, the sweep and frenzy of motion. Earlier, every movement in the village had seemed in slow motion. Now the ambience quickened. "Maybe we are relatives, at that," Cliff conceded. Yet, hospitality aside, I think Cliff found the Sindis disappointingly different from the Sintis.

In the garden city of Lahore, 450 miles north, we luxuriated again in a hotel. Moslem tradition dates the founding of modern Lahore to the 11th century, and to the able governorship of Malik Ayaz—the trusted slave of Ghazni's Sultan Mahmud.

"Wouldn't you know," laughed Cliff, "that a Gypsy like Ayaz would manage to find a campsite like this?"

But Gypsy luck evaded us here. We lacked the proper papers to take our cars into India, and couldn't spare the time to set things right.

"Muskros! Officials!" I growled as we unpacked. We could ship the cars home, but we had set out to drive to India—and we had failed.

"Not really," protested Cliff. "We've been tracing the way my people traveled this Gypsy trail—by caravan and cart and donkey-back. Now I'll be entering the subcontinent just the way my people left it: with nothing but my own two feet."

And, of course, an airline ticket.

A*S WE SORTED OUT THE PEOPLE* around Delhi, we conferred with anthropologists, and even fell among people once officially classified as thieves. For on the advice of Mr. J. H. Chinchalkar, of the All-India Tribal Welfare Association, we observed members of the Sansi —a nomadic, Gypsy-like group.

The Sansis "claim that their ancestors . . . were brave soldiers," writes Professor P. C. Biswas of the University of Delhi. "However . . . they were defeated and had to seek refuge in the neighboring jungles . . . forced to take recourse to looting. . . ." Thus the Sansis explain why the British in 1871 classed them with the 128 Criminal Tribes—a stigma removed by the Indian government in 1952. Now the Sansis—among 23,000,000 people—are officially called "an Ex-criminal Tribe," a term I found not quite deodorized. In a rowdy part of the Paharganj Multani Dhanda section of Delhi, we met an assortment of settled Sansis and other ex-criminals along a route our driver called the "Street of Thieves."

Canopies and clotheslines stretched across the narrow way. Women cooked on smoky charcoal fires along the sidewalk while men reclined on cots—playing cards, smoking, laughing. The street seethed in half-riot, so I had to converse with our driver in an all-out yell.

"Not everyone here steals," the driver shouted. "Some deal in dead animals, for leather. But, of course, crime is a traditional craft." He added knowingly, "You can get anything you want on this street."

"Really?" said Cliff. "Well, all I want is a bath—and *that* isn't here." Later Cliff asked me, a little hurt, whether I thought criminals "might be related to our lot."

"Some people," I said lamely, "have made that suggestion." But I also showed Cliff the disclaimer from Sir George A. Grierson in the 1922 edition of his *Linguistic Survey of India.* After studying the Sansi and other wandering groups, he said, "The language of the gipsies of Europe . . . points toward the extreme North-West of India, and the prevailing opinion amongst scholars seems to be that they have nothing to do with the Indian tribes whose dialects are here under consideration."

A wandering knife grinder in Quetta, Pakistan, beams his astonishment as "Lee Sahib" borrows his pedal-powered whetstone and hones a knife to a fine edge.

The Doms were somewhat different. Some Doms are respectable arti-
sans and artists—like those we had already met—and others are roving
thieves. Yet many Gypsiologists have long believed that the word "Rom"
comes from "Dom." Grierson adds other points: that Doms are a menial
caste, that some "supply fire at cremation or act as executioners; others
are scavengers, and some have taken to basket and cane working." He
notes that long ago Doms "are mentioned in Sanskrit literature as living
by singing and music," and that the word "Dom" may come from the
Sanskrit *damaru,* drum. Yet the Doms "do not possess a dialect of their
own, but use the speech of their neighbors."

So again the Gypsy trail went cold.

"Well, what about the Lohars?" Cliff suggested. The Gaduliya Lohars, or
"cart smiths," of Rajasthan offer an interesting story. Only a few Gypsiologists suggest these traveling smiths are closely related to Romanies.
Their reasons for giving up a settled life and taking to the boat-shaped
bullock carts they now use bear a date too recent for our Gypsies.

"They believe their ancestors belonged to the higher Rajput caste," said
sociologist Satya Pal Ruhela, who had spent many years studying them.
He took us to several Lohar camps in Delhi. "At the Chitorgarh Fort,
they made weapons for the army of a Rajput ruler." But then the army
of Mogul Emperor Akbar attacked in 1568. The fort fell, and the Lohars
escaped. Stunned by the downfall of their beloved stronghold, they took
a vow to observe five taboos until, as they said, "the freedom and glories
of the fort were restored." They would not return to Chitorgarh Fort,
nor live in settled homes, nor light a lamp at night, nor keep a rope for
drawing water from a well, nor carry a cot right side up on their carts.

My eyes confirmed the folktale: Some of the legs of cots still pointed
skyward from the carts. I watched an old Lohar smith at work—his white
beard tied neatly out of the way—beating hot iron into a gate hinge. I
started to sit down on an unused anvil.

"Careful," said Dr. Ruhela. "Don't sit on it, or even touch it with your
shoe. That *eran*—the anvil—is considered holy because it was given to the
Lohars by the god Shiva during their wanderings after the fall of the fort."

Later, I saw an old woman with an empty jar waiting patiently beside a
well for a passerby—a Lohar today is not even *permitted* to draw water
from public wells. I had a rope but no jar, and wanted to help her out, but
didn't quite dare: Lohars refuse water from low-caste leather workers,
launderers, or untouchables. And I, an obvious beefeater with no caste
at all, might not qualify socially to pour. So the Lohar lady and I both
waited for a dipper of water.

"Now what about the Banjaras?" asked Cliff. "Miss Yates said I would
find them the most like my people."

We searched Delhi for two days before finding any Banjaras, called Lam-
banis—salt dealers—in some parts of India. "Hardly surprising," smiled
Mr. Chinchalkar. "Even their name originally meant 'forest dweller.'"
Yet Mr. Chinchalkar sent us at once to some Banjara mat weavers he
knew, the Mehtab Singh family. They lived in a beautifully clean house
with a walled, tree-shaded court, and they invited us to tea. Youngsters
noisily dragged out chairs, and veiled women dithered with cups.

"I am an English Banjara," Cliff told them, to their great delight.

Bruce wanted pictures of the women in traditional costumes, with rings on their toes. They consented and even invited Sheila inside while they changed. "Such a clean house," said Sheila when she emerged.

"Did they keep their faces covered?" asked Bruce.

Sheila blushed. "They didn't have *anything* covered. They stripped and," she paused uncertainly, "they have tattooed stomachs!"

Cliff meantime was finding words in common with Mr. Singh: leaf, tree, wind, old, money, silver, uncle, aunt. The list grew.

"We use our own language in this house—not Hindi," said our host. "Our old people all use this language, but not the young."

So, too, changes the nomadic life of the Banjaras. Tradition says they were once a ruling class that provided warriors for Alexander the Great. Later they turned to selling salt and keeping flocks—until their fortunes worsened and they became nomads, working on farms, bartering in herbs, combs, and livestock. Anthropologist J. P. Juyal of the All-India Nomadic Tribes Association describes the Banjara as "a happy go merry person thinking, 'If today can be enjoyed better why worry for tomorrow?'" Anthropologist V. Raghavaiah adds, "Their women are famous for good looks. . . . Dance and song are ingrained in their marrow and blood."

Banjaras are also found elsewhere in Punjab State, as well as across much of the rest of India. Finally, not far from Agra, we found a Banjara village. We had gone to the ruins of Fatehpur Sikri, a 16th-century capital city built by Akbar, when Cliff said, "Look—a Gypsy bird!" Sure enough, a pied wagtail was wading in the irrigation canal. "We ought to ask about Banjaras camping around here."

So we asked—and instead of a camp, we were directed to Bharkol, a palm-shaded village among fields of sugarcane and wheat. The houses had sloping walls plastered with mud and cow dung—which surprisingly has a fresh, grassy smell—and doors and windows outlined in cubist patterns.

"Yes, we are 200 Banjaras here," said an elder of Bharkol. "Our fathers came from near Jodhpur perhaps 100 years ago. They were haulers of goods with wagons and horses and donkeys, and their women sold needles door to door. But they had no water, so they came here. Now we are farmers. Most of us own land."

Prepackaged popcorn, a gift from photographer Dale, explodes inside its aluminum-foil dome for fascinated Sindi villagers at Kādirpur, Pakistan. The men pocketed samples for their families.

His own riches included ten goats, two buffaloes, and two bullocks.

In the shade of a feathery neem tree, the villagers brought us sugarcane to chew. "That old blind man," said Cliff, pointing to a dark fellow with a white mustache. "He's the image of my grandfather. Exactly."

Now the women—heavily veiled and shy as antelope—showed Sheila their dresses. "They sew bits of shiny tin onto the cloth," Sheila noted.

The sun was sinking on the flat farmlands as we prepared to leave. "Won't you spend the night?" our Banjara friends asked. But we couldn't. Cliff and Sheila were celebrating their silver wedding anniversary—and all of us were packing to leave. It was time for a nostalgic look over our shoulders—at the 13,000 miles we had traveled, at the souvenirs and the addresses of new friends. And at the things we had learned.

We had many unanswered questions, and as I sorted two dozen notebooks and bales of monographs, I read and wondered.

From Washington, researcher Tee Snell had sent us a summary of Gypsy scholarship: "Philologists agree that Europe's Gypsies started out from the northwest of India—including modern western Pakistan. In Iran and Asia Minor some probably straggled behind. Others may have branched off the northern route—those now in Syria, for example.

"But scholars still argue the date the Gypsies left India. Miklosich says 'about the year 1000.' The word 'about' leaves room for speculating that Firdawsi's Luris, or the robber Zotts who brought water buffalo, or some other Indian groups known to have arrived in South Persia before the year 1000 might be the ancestors of our Gypsies."

Then Tee noted that if experts quibble over the timing of the great Gypsy exodus from India, they quarrel strongly over *why* the Gypsies left: Did some catastrophe uproot them, or did they follow their wanderlust? Did they start off free or enslaved? And finally, as scholars sort out the

After finding Gypsies near Agra, the author, photographer Dale, and the Lees visit the Taj Mahal, a goal of many "wanderers" across the globe. The tomb's fragile, cloudlike quality stirred Dale to "work fast, lest it vanish."

modern ethnic groups of Mother India and search for the Gypsies' next-of-kin, they raise their voices in favor of groups like the Doms, Dards, Jats, Sindis — or an unknown people of central India. England's distinguished Sanskrit scholar Sir Ralph L. Turner says the Romany language shows that some 300 years before Christ our Gypsies left central India for northwest India, where they stayed perhaps a thousand years before starting their long move westward.

So, are our Gypsies the heirs of Shah Bahram Gur's musicians or of Mahmud's slaves? If neither of those, then perhaps our Romanies started like the Gaduliya Lohars — with a military defeat and a sacred vow to leave home. Or profanely, like the once-criminal Sansis. Did a powerful ruler lose patience and banish his thieves?

And what about caste — were the early Gypsies pariahs or nobles? Here I consulted Sultan Mahmud's contemporary, the scientist and historian Albiruni, who viewed India at the beginning of the 11th century. Albiruni listed four castes, and then certain craft classes "who are not reckoned amongst any caste" — among them the jugglers and the makers of baskets and shields. Below them, of no caste or craft class, are those like the Doms, who do "dirty work [and] are considered like illegitimate children." But a few pages farther on, I read another comment on caste. I had wondered why Mahmud's Hindu slaves would have fled westward instead of home to Mother India. Now Albiruni reported:

"I have repeatedly been told that when Hindu slaves... escape and return to their country... the Hindus order that they should fast by way of expiation, then they bury them in the dung... and milk of cows... till they get into a state of fermentation.... I have asked the Brahmans if this is true, but they... maintain that there is no expiation possible for such an individual, and that he is never allowed to return into those conditions of life in which he was before he was carried off as a prisoner."

So a runaway Hindu slave, if not already a pariah, could have held onto his old status only if he never returned home. And the wanderers did retain their sense of caste, Afghanistan's Dr. Farhadi says. This may account for the fact that the European Lovara look down on the Kalderash, and the Kalderash look down on the Sintis — and all look down on the gorgios.

"Perhaps types of work, or non-work, and the diversity of physical characteristics among Gypsy bands in Europe — from near black to blond, and hair from horsetail straight to very curly — could indicate the range of castes," Tee suggested.

WITH ALL our inconsistent Gypsy theories spread out, the four of us enjoyed a sumptuous farewell dinner at New Delhi's Ashoka Hotel. I watched a regal headwaiter bow before Clifford Lee. And in that instant I was certain that, whatever caste Gypsies might once have held here, Cliff was now very much the relaxed *raja-rai,* and Lord of Little Egypt. "What's your impression?" I asked him. "Who are your people?" He smiled and said, "Oh, Bart, there are so many *kinds* of Gypsies. I can tell the clan of any Gypsy in Britain just by his particular — and I think vestigial tribal — characteristics. We must have come from many Indian tribes." He had a point: Could musicians, thieves, dancers, animal trainers, clairvoyants, blacksmiths — could such a miscellany *ever* have been one single group in India?

Or did it happen that varied sorts of Indians met and joined forces in old Iran? Some might have been refugees, others wandering remnants of earlier arrivals. Could their dialects, from widely separated centuries, have intermingled—and thus created for Gypsiologists a marvelously compounded mystery?

But there comes a time in the study of Gypsies when a man must abandon the scholar for the advice of poets. Robert Browning wondered about their travels—"a place here, a place there"—and concluded:

> *...I believe they rise out of the ground,*
> *And nowhere else, I take it, are found*
> *With the earth-tint yet so freshly embrowned....*

"We're fascinating devils," said Cliff, "and our mystery remains intact."

It did the hot day we said goodbye in Delhi. The Lees left first—their plane headed toward Australia and a visit with son Ken. Cliff hadn't a single pun, and Sheila didn't trust herself to talk at all.

"I remember this feeling from my boyhood," said Cliff, "when we'd traveled and camped with other families for a while, and then they went their own way. Now I know how you must feel, Bart, and you, Bruce. Being the last to leave the campsite—that's the loneliest feeling on earth."

We waved, and the long journey was almost over. As Bruce and I waited in the airport, I found my copy of Dora Yates's memoirs. The pages fell open—unnervingly—to her recollections of a "piece of luck in 1908" when she found "Ithal Lee and his family, camped in a green lane." I felt a prickling sensation as I read of Cliff's grandfather Ithal. Dr. Yates quoted his comments on India—and how "he had heard that the *foki* there understood words like *pani* for 'water'...." And then old Ithal confessed "his greatest ambition was to take his caravan to India...."

I thought about baht and patrins and dukkeripen. And then, to restore sweet reason, I reached into my pocket to touch a green Rumanian ring.

*W*oman of the Brahui nomads of Baluchistan firmly grips her camel's tether. At left, a distant train chugs past goatherds.

*B*rahui tribesmen drive donkeys and camels through Pakistan's arid
Bolan Pass, used for centuries by traders, nomad tribes, and wandering
Gypsies. Rude upright stones (above) mark wayside graves.

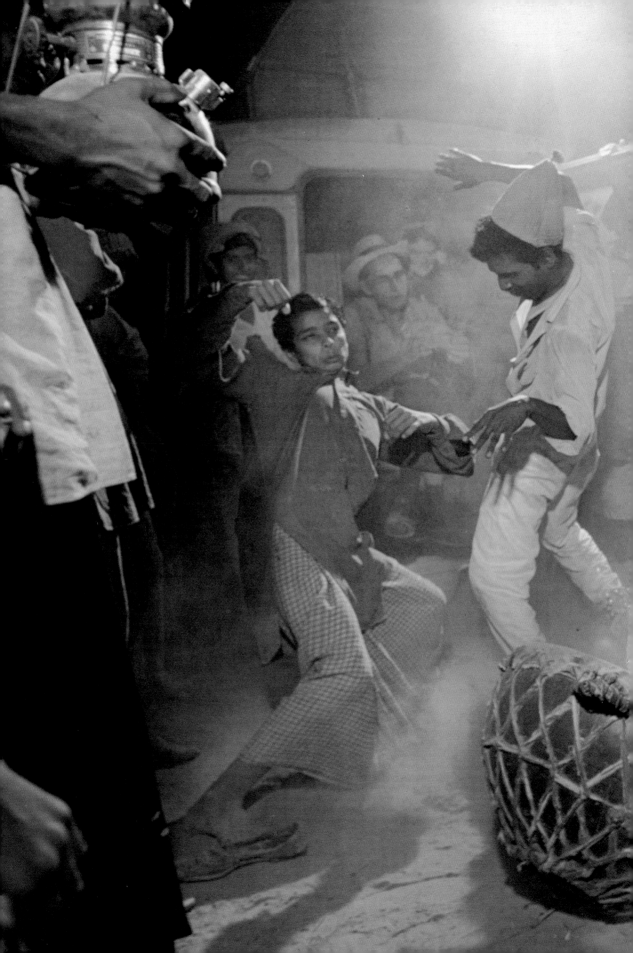

S*indi people of Pakistan resemble Sinti*

Gypsies of Europe in name and appearance, but little else. At the Sindi

village of Kādirpur near the Indus, piercing eyes gleam in the

bearded face of a visitor from a nearby settlement (right); children

(below) smile shyly. Preceding pages: Sindi men dance to the beat

of kettle-like drums, or dhol. *Following pages: A driver steadies*

his oxen beside mud-brick buildings lining a Kādirpur street.

Famous throughout India for their beauty, women
of the Banjara tribe gossip in the village of Bharkol, southwest of Agra.
Clifford Lee found the Banjaras much like his own people in England.
As a woman adjusts her patterned sari (above), bangles clink
down her elaborately tattooed hand and wrist. Red paint (below)
outlines openings in walls plastered with mud and cow dung.

𝓑anjara basket maker of New Delhi (right) trims reeds to length;
like many tribeswomen, she wears no veil. A Banjara
man seeks the shade during the heat of the midday sun.

$\mathcal{B}$oat-shaped cart carries the belongings of a Gaduliya Lohar;

400 years ago, folklore says, her people vowed to shun settled homes.

A boy spends a moment in curious reflection. Gold brightens a woman's smile.

*C*hildren jostle a sacred cow to get into the picture
in a rowdy area of Delhi, where the author's taxi driver
told him, "You can get anything you want on this street." A printed
cotton canopy shades card players (right) in this
neighborhood of the Sansi, a Gypsy-like group once a
"Criminal Tribe" and now officially numbered among "Ex-criminal Tribes."

Cliff Lee bids farewell to a New Delhi snake charmer
as their paths, having touched briefly, separate again.

After his trip to India — the fulfillment of a years-
long dream — Lee could say with assurance,
"Mandi si dadesko tem — *I have a paternal land." He found,*
as scholars have noted, many Hindi words virtually the
same in his Romany tongue. But deeper impressions proved
more convincing: "the subtle nuances of behavior which a
thousand-year exile from India could not wash away."

Index

Illustrations references, including legends, appear in *italics*.

Additional references

The reader may wish to refer to the following NATIONAL GEOGRAPHIC articles for additional reading and to check the Cumulative Index before 1940 for other related material:

GYPSIES: "Gypsy Cave Dwellers of Andalusia (Spain)," October 1957; Eugene L. Kammerman, "The Camargue, Land of the Cowboys and Gypsies," May 1956; Dorothea Sheats (Mrs. Stuart E. Jones), "I Walked Some Irish Miles," May 1951; Luis Marden, "Speaking of Spain," April 1950.
AFGHANISTAN: Thomas J. Abercrombie, "Afghanistan: Crossroad of Conquerors," September 1968; Tay and Lowell Thomas, Jr., "Sky Road East," January 1960; William O. Douglas, "West from the Khyber Pass," July 1958; Maynard Owen Williams, "Back to Afghanistan," October 1946.
CZECHOSLOVAKIA: Edward J. Linehan, "Czechoslovakia: The Dream and the Reality," February 1968.
ENGLAND: Louis B. Wright, "The World of Elizabeth I," November 1968.
GERMANY: William Graves, "The Rhine: Europe's River of Legend," April 1967.
GREECE: Kenneth F. Weaver, "Athens: Her Golden Past Still Lights the World," July 1963.
INDIA: John Scofield, "India in Crisis," May 1963; Anthony and Georgette Dickey Chapelle, "New Life for India's Villagers," April 1956; Phillips Talbot, "Delhi, Capital of a New Dominion," November 1947; Maynard Owen Williams, "South of Khyber Pass," April 1946; Lord Halifax, "India—Yesterday, Today and Tomorrow," October 1943.
IRAN: Edward J. Linehan, "Old-New Iran, Next Door to Russia," January 1961; Jean and Franc Shor, "We Dwelt in Kashgai Tents," June 1952; George W. Long, "Journey into Troubled Iran," October 1951.
PAKISTAN: Bern Keating, "Pakistan: Problems of a Two-Part Land," January 1967; Jean and Franc Shor, "Pakistan, New Nation in an Old Land," November 1952.
RUMANIA: Dan Dimancescu, "Americans Afoot in Rumania," June 1969.
TURKEY: Nan and James W. Borton, "Turkey," September 1964; Kenneth M. Setton, "A New Look at Medieval Europe," December 1962; Maynard Owen Williams, "Turkey Paves the Path of Progress," August 1951; and "The Turkish Republic Comes of Age," May 1945; "Alert Anatolia," April 1944.
YUGOSLAVIA: Robert Paul Jordan, "Yugoslavia, Six Republics in One," May 1970; "Restive Heartland: The Balkans," February 1962; Ethel Chamberlain Porter, "The Clock Turns Back in Yugoslavia: The Fortified Monastery of Mountain-girt Dečani Survives Its Six Hundredth Birthday," April 1944.
MISCELLANEOUS: Melville Bell Grosvenor, "Journey into the Age of Chivalry," October 1969; Helen and Frank Schreider, "In the Footsteps of Alexander the Great," January 1968; William Slade Backer, "Down the Danube by Canoe," July 1965; Jean and Franc Shor, "Athens to Istanbul," January 1956; Franc Shor, "In the Crusaders' Footsteps," June 1962.

Composition for *Gypsies: Wanderers of the World* by National Geographic's Phototypo-
graphic Division, John E. McConnell, Manager. Printed and bound by Fawcett Printing
Corp., Rockville, Md. Color separations by Beck Engraving Co., Philadelphia, Pa.; Color-
graphics, Inc., Beltsville, Md.; Graphic Color Plate, Inc., Stamford, Conn.; The Lanman
Co., Alexandria, Va.; McCall Printing Co., Charlotte, N.C.; Printing Service Co., Dayton,
Ohio; and Progressive Color Corp., Rockville, Md.

Ces pauures gueux pleins de bonaduētures
Ne portent rien que des Choses futures.

"These ragged tramps, full of futures to sell, bear little but the words of the fortunes